databook
& price guide

Firebird
1967-1978

compiled by
r. perry zavitz

BOOKMAN PUBLISHING

Baltimore, Maryland

CONTENTS

INTRODUCTION...................................... 4

1967..6

1968.. 17

1969.. 27

1970.. 38

1971.. 47

1972.. 57

1973.. 67

1974.. 77

1975.. 87

1976.. 97

1977..106

1978.. 118

INTRODUCTION

Welcome to the second, revised edition of the Firebird Databook and Price Guide. This is a unique type of publication for Firebird enthusiasts. It offers data on models, production, popular options, prices (when the cars were new and as current collectibles) and a host of other subjects of interest. Best of all, this useful information is presented in a handy, pocket-size format that can be easily carried to car shows, car dealers--wherever a quick reference source is required.

The information contained in this volume was carefully compiled from a wide variety of sources, mostly dating from when the cars were new and most of it hard to find today. Factory data was tapped when possible, but trade journals, enthusiast publications and other reliable sources were also used. We believe that the data contained here is correct, but, in the event that discrepancies have crept in, we would appreciate hearing from our readers. Our one goal is to have the most accurate possible source of essential Firebird information.

ABOUT THE PRICE DATA

A few words are in order regarding the annual "Price Data" sections. These are sure to be among the most valuable and best read sections, especially the contemporary values.

The first question an owner of a collectible car asks always seems to be, "What is my car worth?" The only meaningful reply is that any car is worth exactly what you can get for it. A lot depends on whether the car is being sold in a hurry; an owner may have to be patient in order to get a good price. Prices vary from region to region, too, and seasonally, as well. It also makes a difference who is doing the selling. Is it a private party who does not know much about Firebird values or a dealer who is determined to get absolute top dollar? In short, the actual sale price of any given car could vary by thousands of dollars in different circumstances. Consequently, price guides, such as this one, should be used as guidelines, not Holy Writ. However, you have to start somewhere and we believe the prices contained in this volume are good "ballpark" estimates of what the various models are fetching as we go to press.

As with most price guides, we have used five categories to describe the condition of each car. They are as follows:

BEST RESTORATION: A car of the very highest caliber. An original car in showroom condition could also meet this standard.

VERY GOOD: Minimal problems. Possibly a good (but not quite perfect) restoration or a very good-to-excellent original.

GOOD: Complete and fully operable, but showing moderate wear. Possibly a good original car, or a poorer (or older) restoration.

FAIR: Deteriorated but functional. This is a car that runs, but needs plenty of work, although it may be reasonably presentable to the casual eye.

POOR: A fixer-upper. This car may or may not be running, but, in any case, needs complete restoration. This category does not include cars unfit for restoration.

We hope you find this new and revised edition a valuable addition to your Firebird library. We appreciate the comments and suggestions of those who wrote in concerning the first edition. We especially thank GM's John Sawruk who supplied much important material, making this edition even better than the old one.

Again, our goal is to be as accurate as possible. We would appreciate hearing about any lapses or any comments or suggestions our readers may have. Please address all correspondence to:

Bookman Publishing
P.O. Box 13492
Baltimore, MD 21203

FIREBIRD SPRINT – COUPE

FIREBIRD 400 – COUPE

FIREBIRD SPRINT – CONVERTIBLE

FIREBIRD 400 – COUPE

Physical Features

Although late in offering a so-called ponycar, Pontiac's Firebird was a popular entry. Its body was basically similar to Chevrolet's Camaro, but mechanically there was nothing borrowed. The smallest engine was Pontiac's overhead cam 230 cid 6-cylinder motor which was available in two potencies. Its smallest V-8 was Pontiac's 326 cid motor, also offered in two power ratings. Likewise, Pontiac's 400 cid V-8 was available in two versions. One had a conventional 4-barrel carburetor and the other added Ram Air. The horsepower figure for each was the same, officially, but in actual performance, the Ram Air had a slight edge. Firebird was offered in hardtop and convertible bodies in only one series. The more powerful OHC six was called Sprint, the milder 326 was called 326, the more potent was labelled the HO and 400 referred to the 400 cid powered Firebirds with or without Ram Air. The HO and Sprint models had racing stripes along the sides incorporating those designations. The 400 had its displacement marked on the rear deck.

Observations

Pontiac was about the last to introduce a ponycar, a compact sized, sporty, performance vehicle. It got off to an excellent start as almost 95,000 Firebirds were sold during calendar 1967. The Firebird did not debut until late February and it accounted for over 11% of Pontiac sales for the calendar year, which helped that division to score an increase.

VIN NUMBERS

Vehicle Identification Number: 223( )7( )( )00001 and up
Explanation:
First symbol: GM division: Pontiac = 2
Second & third symbols: Series number: Firebird = 23
Fourth & fifth symbols: Body code:
    hardtop = 37
    convertible = 67
Sixth symbol: Last digit of model year
Seventh symbol: Letter indicating assembly plant
Eighth symbol: Number of cylinders:
    6 cyl = 6
    V-8 = 1
Ninth to thirteenth symbol: Sequential production number

PRODUCTION TOTALS

Body Type	Units	Percent
hardtop	67032	81.2
convertible	15528	18.8
Total	82560	100.0

Engine Installations

6 cyl	17664	21.4
V-8	64896	78.6

DRIVETRAIN DATA

base model, standard
Cylinder Configuration:	Inline
Number of Cylinders:	6
Cylinder Bore (in):	3.875
Cylinder Stroke (in):	3.25
Displacement (cu in):	230.0
Carburetion:	1 1-bbl
Carburetor Make:	Rochester
Carburetor Model:	BV
Compression Ratio:	9.0
Brake Horsepower:	165
RPM @ Maximum Hp:	4700
Torque, ft-lb:	216
RPM @ Maximum Torque:	2600

Standard for Sprint
Cylinder Configuration:	Inline
Number of Cylinders:	6
Cylinder Bore (in):	3.875
Cylinder Stroke (in):	3.25
Displacement (cu in):	230.0
Carburetion:	1 4-bbl
Carburetor Make:	Rochester
Carburetor Model:	4MV
Compression Ratio:	10.5
Brake Horsepower:	215
RPM @ Maximum Hp:	5200
Torque, ft-lb:	250
RPM @ Maximum Torque:	4800

Standard for 326

Cylinder Configuration:	V
Number of Cylinders:	8
Cylinder Bore (in):	3.72
Cylinder Stroke (in):	3.75
Displacement (cu in):	326.1
Carburetion:	1 2-bbl
Carburetor Make:	Rochester
Carburetor Model:	2GC
Compression Ratio:	9.2
Brake Horsepower:	250
RPM @ Maximum Hp:	4600
Torque, ft-lb:	333
RPM @ Maximum Torque:	2800

Standard for HO

Cylinder Configuration:	V
Number of Cylinders:	8
Cylinder Bore (in):	3.72
Cylinder Stroke (in):	3.75
Displacement (cu in):	326.1
Carburetion:	1 4-bbl
Carburetor Make:	Carter
Carburetor Model:	AFB
Compression Ratio:	10.5
Brake Horsepower:	285
RPM @ Maximum Hp:	5000
Torque, ft-lb:	359
RPM @ Maximum Torque:	3200

Standard for 400

Cylinder Configuration:	V
Number of Cylinders:	8
Cylinder Bore (in):	4.12
Cylinder Stroke (in):	3.75
Displacement (cu in):	400.0
Carburetion:	1 4-bbl
Carburetor Make:	Rochester
Carburetor Model:	4MV
Compression Ratio:	10.75
Brake Horsepower:	325
RPM @ Maximum Hp:	4800
Torque, ft-lb:	410
RPM @ Maximum Torque:	3400

Optional

Cylinder Configuration:	V
Number of Cylinders:	8
Cylinder Bore (in):	4.12
Cylinder Stroke (in):	3.75
Displacement (cu in):	400.0
Carburetion:	1 4-bbl
Carburetor Make:	Rochester
Carburetor Model:	4MV
Compression Ratio:	10.75
Brake Horsepower:	325
RPM @ Maximum Hp:	5200
Torque, ft-lb:	410
RPM @ Maximum Torque:	3800

TRANSMISSIONS

Model	base	Sprint	326	HO	400
Standard:	3-spdM	3-spdM	3-spdM	3-spdM	3-spdM
Shift Location:	column	floor	column	column	floor
Optional:	2-spdA	2-spdA	2-spdA	2-spdA	3-spdA
	--	4-spdM	4-spdM	4-spdM	4-spdM

Transmission Ratios

	3-spdM		4-spdM	2-spdA	3-spdA
availabilities:	(b)	(a)	(b)	(f)	400
first:	2.85	2.54	2.52	1.76	2.48
second:	1.68	1.50	1.88	1.00	1.48
third:	1.00	1.00	1.46	--	1.00
fourth:	--	--	1.00	--	--
reverse:	2.95	2.63	2.59	1.76	2.08

b = only base model; a = all but base model; f = all but 400

Rear Axle Ratios

Engine Hp:	165	215	250	285	325
Standard (M/T):	3.08	3.55	3.23	3.36	3.36
Standard (A/T):	2.56	3.23	2.56	3.23	3.08
Optional:	2.93(a)	2.78	2.93	3.55	3.23(c)
	3.23(c)	3.23(c)	3.08	3.90	3.55
	3.36				3.90(r)
					4.33(r)

a = with automatic; c = with air-conditioning; r = with Ram Air

EXTERIOR DATA

	hardtop	convertible
Overall Length (in):	188.8	188.8
Overall Width (in):	72.8	72.6
Overall Height (in):	51.5	51.4
Wheelbase (in):	108.1	108.1

Shipping Weight (lb):

base	2955	3247
Sprint	3010	3302
326	3123	3415

EXTERIOR FINISHES

Color	Code	Color	Code
Cameo Ivory	C	Montreux Blue	D
Fathom Blue	E	Tyrol Blue	F
Signet Gold	G	Linden Green	H
Gulf Turquoise	K	Mariner Turquoise	L
Burgundy	N	Coronado Gold	O
Silverglaze	P	Verdoro Green	Q
Regimental Red	R	Champagne	S
Mayfair Maize	Y	Montego Cream*	T
Plum Mist*	M	Black*	A

*Extra cost at $10.50

UPHOLSTERY

Material	Color	Code		Recommended Exterior Colors
Morrokide	Blue	250	255*	C,D,E,F,P
buckets	Gold	251	257*	C,G,O,Q,S,Y
	Red	252	258*	C,N,P,R
	Black	253	259*	any color
	Parchment	254	260*	any color
	Turquoise		256*	C,K,L,P

*Custom interiors with only cameo ivory and tyrol blue

Convertible Tops		Cordova Tops	
Color	Code	Color	Code
Ivory	1	Ivory	1
Black	2	Black	2
Blue	4	Cream	7
Turquoise	5		
Cream	7		

PRICE DATA

Base Price	hardtop	convertible
base	2666	2903
Sprint	2782	3019
326	2761	2998
HO	2825	3062
400	2777	3177

CURRENT VALUE (approximate)

Model Condition		Best	Very Good	Good	Fair	Poor
base	hardtop	5000	3500	2500	1500	750
	convertible	6200	4340	3100	1860	930
Sprint & V-8s	hardtop	5500	3850	2750	1650	825
	convertible	7700	5390	3850	2310	1155
Ram Air	hardtop	6500	4550	3250	1950	975
	convertible	8500	5950	4250	2550	1275

POPULAR FACTORY OPTIONS

Item	Code	Price (nearest $)	
Air-conditioning	582	356	
Brakes, Disc	521	63	
Clock, Electric	474	16	
Console	472	47	
Cruise Control	441	53	
Differential, Safe-T-Track	731	42	
Exhaust, Dual	481	30	(326 only, std on HO & 400)
Exhaust Tailpipe Extensions	482	20	
Glass, Tinted	531	30	
Glass, Tinted, windshield only	532	21	
Handling Package	621	9	
Head Rests	572	53	

Instruments, Rally & Hood Tach	444	32
Mirror, remote control	394	9
Power Brakes, Drum	502	42
Power Steering	501	95
Power Top	544	53	(conv. only)
Power Windows	551	100
Radio, Pushbutton	342	61
Radio, AM/FM	344	134
Rear Seat, fold-down	654	37
Rear Speaker	351	16
Rear Window Defogger	374	21
Seat Belts, custom front & rear	431	6
Shoulder Straps, front	434	23
Speedometer, Safeguard	442	11
Steering Wheel, deluxe	462	12
Steering Wheel, custom	471	30
Steering Wheel, tilt	504	42
Tachometer, hood-mounted	704	63
Tape, Stereo	354	128
Transmission, 3-spd manual floor		42
Transmission, 4-speed manual		184
Transmission, 2-speed A Turbo Hydramatic		184
Trunk Lid Remote Control		13
Vinyl Roof	STV	84
Wheel Discs, deluxe	461	17
Wheel Discs, custom	458	19
Wheel Discs, wire	452	53
Wheels, Rally II	453	53
Wheels, Rally I	454	40

PERFORMANCE DATA

Source:	MOTOR TREND	MOTOR TREND	MOTOR TREND
Engine Hp:	285	325	325*
Transmission:	2-spdA	4-spdM	3-spdA
Rear Axle Ratio:	nr	nr	nr
0 to 60 Time (secs):	7.8	6.7	6.4
1/4 Mile Time (secs):	16.0	14.5	14.3
1/4 Mile Speed (mph):	90	98	100.3
Maximum Speed (mph):	nr	nr	nr
60 to 0 Braking Distance (ft):	nr	nr	nr
MPG (city):	nr	12.7	nr
MPG (highway):	nr	14.7	nr
MPG (combined):	nr	nr	nr

* Ram Air
nr = not reported

Physical Features

Few appearance changes were made to the Firebird after its initial short year. Only the deletion of side vent windows and the addition of side marker lights served to distinguish a 1968 model from 1967 to the knowledgeable observer (although some early models had frosted Firebirds in the window glass where the vent used to be). Many changes were made to the engines, generally resulting in more power. The OHC-6 received a slightly larger bore, bringing its displacement to 250 cubic inches. That increased its horsepower by 10 in base form, but no change in output was made to the already more powerful Sprint. Likewise, the 326 V-8 had its bore increased, resulting in a displacement of 354 cubic inches. It was offically designated as a 350 cubic inch engine and the models so equipped were called Firebird 350s. The Firebird HO used a more powerful version of this engine. The 400 had a choice of three engines--the base 400 cid V-8, an HO version that developed just 5 more horsepower and the Ram Air version which rated the same as the HO.

Observations

Production of the Firebird rose considerably, but there was a complete model year for 1968, compared to only a partial model run for the 1967 models.

Firebird HO

18

VIN NUMBERS

Vehicle Identification Number: 223( )8( )( )00001 and up
Explanation:
First symbol: GM division: Pontiac = 2
Second & third symbols: Series number: Firebird = 23
Fourth & fifth symbols: Body code:
    hardtop = 37
    convertible = 67
Sixth symbol: Last digit of model year
Seventh symbol: Letter indicating assembly plant
Eighth symbol: Number of cylinders:
    6 cyl = 6
    V-8 = 1
Ninth to thirteenth symbol: Sequential production number

PRODUCTION TOTALS

Body Type	Units	%
hardtop	90152	84.2
convertible	16960	15.8
Total	107112	100.0

Engine Installations

6 cyl	18494	17.3
V-8	88618	82.7

DRIVETRAIN DATA

base model, standard

Cylinder Configuration:	Inline
Number of Cylinders:	6
Cylinder Bore (in):	3.875
Cylinder Stroke (in):	3.53
Displacement (cu in):	249.8
Carburetion:	1 1-bbl
Carburetor Make:	Rochester
Carburetor Model:	BV
Compression Ratio:	9.0
Brake Horsepower:	175
RPM @ Maximum Hp:	4800
Torque, ft-lb:	240
RPM @ Maximum Torque:	2600

Sprint Option:

Cylinder Configuration:	Inline
Number of Cylinders:	6
Cylinder Bore (in):	3.875
Cylinder Stroke (in):	3.53
Displacement (cu in):	249.8
Carburetion:	1 4-bbl
Carburetor Make:	Rochester
Carburetor Model:	4MV
Compression Ratio:	10.5
Brake Horsepower:	215
RPM @ Maximum Hp:	5200
Torque, ft-lb:	255
RPM @ Maximum Torque:	3800

326 Option:
Cylinder Configuration: V
Number of Cylinders: 8
Cylinder Bore (in):   3.875
Cylinder Stroke (in):   3.75
Displacement (cu in):   353.8
Carburetion: 1 2-bbl
Carburetor Make: Rochester
Carburetor Model: 2GV
Compression Ratio: 9.2
Brake Horsepower: 265
RPM @ Maximum Hp: 4600
Torque, ft-lb: 355
RPM @ Maximum Torque: 2800

400 HO Option:
Cylinder Configuration: V
Number of Cylinders: 8
Cylinder Bore (in):   412
Cylinder Stroke (in):   3.75
Displacement (cu in):   400.0
Carburetion: 1 4-bbl
Carburetor Make: Rochester
Carburetor Model: 4MV
Compression Ratio: 10.75
Brake Horsepower: 335
RPM @ Maximum Hp: 5000
Torque, ft-lb: 430
RPM @ Maximum Torque: 3400

400 Ram Air Option:

Cylinder Configuration:	V
Number of Cylinders:	8
Cylinder Bore (in):	4.12
Cylinder Stroke (in):	3.75
Displacement (cu in):	400.0
Carburetion:	1 4-bbl
Carburetor Make:	Rochester
Carburetor Model:	4MV
Compression Ratio:	10.75
Brake Horsepower:	335
RPM @ Maximum Hp:	5300
Torque, ft-lb:	430
RPM @ Maximum Torque:	3600

TRANSMISSIONS

Engine Option:	base	Sprint	326	HO	400 (all)
Standard:	3-spdM	3-spdM	3-spdM	3-spdM	3-spdM HD
Shift Location:	column	floor	column	column	floor
Optional:	2-spdA	2-spdA	2-spdA	2-spdA	3-spdA
	4-spdM	3-spdM HD	3-spdM HD	3-spdM HD	4-spdM
		4-spdM	4-spdM	4-spdM	

Transmission Ratios

	3-spdM		4-spdM		2-spdA	3-spdA
availabilities:	(b)	(a)	(b)	(a)	(f)	400
first:	2.85	2.54	2.52	2.85	1.76	2.42
second:	1.68	1.50	1.88	2.02	1.00	1.61
third:	1.00	1.00	1.46	1.35	--	1.00
fourth:	--	--	1.00	1.00	--	--
reverse:	2.95	2.63	2.59	2.85	1.76	2.33

b = only base model; a = all but base model; f = all but 400

Rear Axle Ratios

Engine Hp:	175	215	265	320	330	335	335*
Standard (M/T):	3.55	3.55(n)	3.23	3.36	3.36(n)	3.36(n)	3.90(n)
Standard (A/T):	3.23	3.23	2.56	3.23	3.08	3.08	3.90(n)
Optional:		2.41(a,n)	2.78(a,n)		2.78(c)		
2.78(a,c)		2.56(a,)	2.56(a,c)	4.33(a)			
		3.08	3.55(a,n)	2.93(a,n)	3.55(n)		
3.23(a,n)		3.55(a,)					
		3.23(c)		3.08(n)	3.90		
3.55(a,c)		3.90(a,n)					
						3.90(a,n)	4.33(a)
						4.33(a)	

a = with automatic; c = with air-conditioning; n = not with air-conditioning

EXTERIOR DATA

	hardtop	convertible
Overall Length (in):	188.8	188.8
Overall Width (in):	72.8	72.6
Overall Height (in):	50.0	49.9
Wheelbase (in):	108.1	108.1

Shipping Weight (lb):

base	3061	3346
350	3224	3509

EXTERIOR FINISHES

Color	Code	Color	Code
Starlight Black	A	Cameo Ivory	C
Alpine Blue	D	Aegena Blue	E
Nordic Blue	F	April Gold	G
Meridian Turquoise	K	Aleutian Blue	L
Flambeau Burgundy	N	Springmist Green	P
Verdoro Green	Q	Solar Red	R
Primavera Beige	T	Nightshade Green	V
Mayfair Maize	Y		

UPHOLSTERY

Seats	Color	Code		Recommended Exterior Colors
bench	Black	272	269*	any color
	Parchment	273	275*	any color
bucket	Teal	250	255*	A,C,D,E,F,L
	Gold	251	257*	A,C,G,Q,T
	Red	252	258*	A,C,N,R
	Black	253	259*	any color
	Turquoise	261	256*	A,C,K
	Parchment	262	260*	any color

*Custom interiors

PRICE DATA

Base Price	hardtop	convertible
base	2781	2996
Sprint	2897	3112
350	2887	3102
HO	3067	3248
400	3054	3269
Ram Air	3397	3612

CURRENT VALUE (approximate)

Model Condition		Best	Very Good	Good	Fair	Poor
base	hardtop	4500	3150	2250	1350	675
	convertible	5700	3990	2850	1710	855
Sprint & V-8s	hardtop	5000	3500	2500	1500	750
	convertible	7200	5040	3600	2160	1080
Ram Air	hardtop	6000	4200	3000	1800	900
	convertible	8200	5740	4100	2460	1230

* Add 50% for Ram Air II

POPULAR FACTORY OPTIONS

Item	Code	Price (nearest $)	
Air-conditioning	582	360	
Brakes, Disc	521	63	
Clock, Electric	474	16	
Console	472	51	
Cruise Control	441	53	
Deck Lid Release	492	14	
Differential, Safe-T-Track	361	42	
Engine, Ram Air	616		(400 only)
Exhaust, Dual	481	31	
Exhaust Tailpipe Extensions	482	21	
Glass, Tinted	531	31	
Glass, Tinted, windshield only	532	21	
Handling Package	621	9	
Head Rests	572	42	
Instruments, Rally & Hood Tach	444	82	
Mirror, remote control	394	7	
Power Brakes	502	42	
Power Brakes, Disc	512	63	
Power Steering	501	95	
Power Top	544	53	(conv. only)
Power Windows	551	100	
Radio, Pushbutton	342	61	
Radio, AM/FM	344	134	
Rally Stripes	494	15	
Rear Seat, fold-down	604	42	
Rear Speaker	391	16	
Rear Window Defogger	404	21	
Seat Belts, custom front & rear	431	13	
Shoulder Straps, front	754	26	
Speedometer, Safeguard	442	16	
Steering Wheel, Deluxe	462	15	
Steering Wheel, Custom Sports	471	45	
Steering Wheel, tilt	504	42	

Tachometer, hood-mounted	434	63
Tape, Stereo	394	134
Transmission, 3-speed manual	356	42
Transmission, 4-speed manual	358	184
Transmission, 2-speed automatic	352	195
Vinyl Roof	STV	84
Wheel Discs, Deluxe	461	21
Wheel Discs, Custom	458	41
Wheel Discs, wire	452	74
Wheels, Rally II	453	84
Wheels, Rally I	454	61

PERFORMANCE DATA

Source:	WORLD CAR	MOTOR TREND	MOTOR TREND
Engine Hp:	330	325	325
Transmission:	3-spdM	4-spdM	3-spdM
Rear Axle Ratio:	nr	nr	nr
0 to 60 Time (secs):	nr	nr	nr
1/4 Mile Time (secs):	nr	14.05	13.99
1/4 Mile Speed (mph):	nr	102.85	105.01
Maximum Speed (mph):	122	nr	nr
65 to 0 Braking Distance (ft):	nr	nr	nr
MPG (city):	nr	nr	nr
MPG (highway):	nr	nr	nr
MPG (combined):	12	nr	nr

nr = not reported

Physical Features

The first styling change of consequence was made to the 1969 Firebird. It still used the same body, but the front end was revised. The grille, in Pontiac tradition, was in two parts--each a chrome-framed rectangle. Now the headlights were outside the grille assembly. Engines underwent little change. Power was up slightly for the HO option and the Ram Air 400. To be precise, this was the Ram Air IV engine. Actually, the 400 HO engine was given Ram Air (sometimes called Ram Air III). The most significant change in 1969 was a late season introduction of the Trans Am option. This was intended to parallel The Judge in Pontiac's GTO line. The few Trans Ams produced were white with two blue racing stripes over the hood, roof and rear deck. The Ram Air III engine was standard, but the IV was installed in a few. The option included a rear deck spoiler and other performance and handling goodies. The blue Trans Am name was placed on the front fenders.

Observations

As with all ponycars, sales during 1969 were sluggish. Firebird registration tumbled about 36%. In overall Pontiac sales, it amounted to a little more than 7%. Not visible in the production statistics was the move that Pontiac made that strengthened Firebird's desirability. That was the introduction of the Trans Am. Though less than 700 were built for 1969, it went on in future years to become Firebird's most popular version.

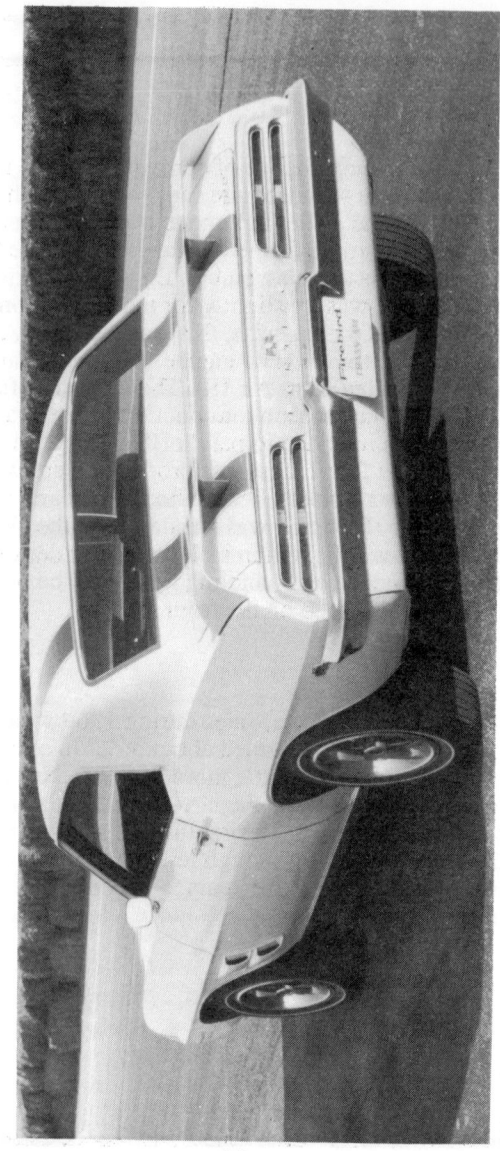

Firebird Trans Am

VIN NUMBERS

Vehicle Identification Number: 223( )9( )( )00001 and up
Explanation:
First symbol: GM division: Pontiac = 2
Second & third symbols: Series number: Firebird = 23
Fourth & fifth symbols: Body code:
　　hardtop = 37
　　convertible = 67
Sixth symbol: Last digit of model year
Seventh symbol: Letter indicating assembly plant
Eighth symbol: Number of cylinders:
　　6 cyl = 6
　　V-8 = 1
Ninth to thirteenth symbol: Sequential production number

PRODUCTION TOTALS

Body Type	Units	Percent
hardtop	75362	85.9
convertible	11649	13.3
Trans Am ht	689	0.8
Trans Am conv	8	0.0
Total	87708	100.0

Manual Transmissions	20840	23.8
Auto Transmissions	66868	76.2

Trans Am			
hardtop	Ram Air III & A/T	114	16.4
	Ram Air III & M/T	520	74.6
	Ram Air IV & A/T	9	1.3
	Ram Air IV & M/T	46	6.6
convertible	Ram Air III & A/T	4	0.6
	Ram Air IV & M/T	4	0.6
Total		697	100.0#

May not total exactly 100 due to rounding

DRIVETRAIN DATA

base model, standard
Cylinder Configuration:	Inline
Number of Cylinders:	6
Cylinder Bore (in):	3.875
Cylinder Stroke (in):	3.53
Displacement (cu in):	249.8
Carburetion:	1 1-bbl
Carburetor Make:	Rochester
Carburetor Model:	BV
Compression Ratio:	9.0
Brake Horsepower:	175
RPM @ Maximum Hp:	4800
Torque, ft-lb:	240
RPM @ Maximum Torque:	2600

Sprint Option
Cylinder Configuration:	Inline
Number of Cylinders:	6
Cylinder Bore (in):	3.875
Cylinder Stroke (in):	3.53
Displacement (cu in):	249.8
Carburetion:	1 4-bbl
Carburetor Make:	Rochester
Carburetor Model:	4MV
Compression Ratio:	10.5
Brake Horsepower:	215
RPM @ Maximum Hp:	5200
Torque, ft-lb:	255
RPM @ Maximum Torque:	3800

326 Option

Cylinder Configuration:	V
Number of Cylinders:	8
Cylinder Bore (in):	3.875
Cylinder Stroke (in):	3.75
Displacement (cu in):	353.8
Carburetion:	1 2-bbl
Carburetor Make:	Rochester
Carburetor Model:	2GV
Compression Ratio:	9.2
Brake Horsepower:	265
RPM @ Maximum Hp:	4600
Torque, ft-lb:	355
RPM @ Maximum Torque:	2800

HO Option

Cylinder Configuration:	V
Number of Cylinders:	8
Cylinder Bore (in):	3.875
Cylinder Stroke (in):	3.75
Displacement (cu in):	353.8
Carburetion:	1 4-bbl
Carburetor Make:	Rochester
Carburetor Model:	4MV
Compression Ratio:	10.5
Brake Horsepower:	325
RPM @ Maximum Hp:	5100
Torque, ft-lb:	380
RPM @ Maximum Torque:	3200

400 Option

Cylinder Configuration:	V
Number of Cylinders:	8
Cylinder Bore (in):	412
Cylinder Stroke (in):	3.75
Displacement (cu in):	400.0
Carburetion:	1 4-bbl
Carburetor Make:	Rochester
Carburetor Model:	4MV
Compression Ratio:	10.75
Brake Horsepower:	330
RPM @ Maximum Hp:	4800
Torque, ft-lb:	430
RPM @ Maximum Torque:	3300

400 HO Option

Cylinder Configuration:	V
Number of Cylinders:	8
Cylinder Bore (in):	412
Cylinder Stroke (in):	3.75
Displacement (cu in):	400.0
Carburetion:	1 4-bbl
Carburetor Make:	Rochester
Carburetor Model:	4MV
Compression Ratio:	10.75
Brake Horsepower:	335
RPM @ Maximum Hp:	5000
Torque, ft-lb:	430
RPM @ Maximum Torque:	3400

400 Ram Air Option

Cylinder Configuration:	V
Number of Cylinders:	8
Cylinder Bore (in):	4.12
Cylinder Stroke (in):	3.75
Displacement (cu in):	400.0
Carburetion:	1 4-bbl
Carburetor Make:	Rochester
Carburetor Model:	4MV
Compression Ratio:	10.75
Brake Horsepower:	335
RPM @ Maximum Hp:	5400
Torque, ft-lb:	430
RPM @ Maximum Torque:	3700

TRANSMISSIONS

Engine Option:	base	Sprint	350	HO
Standard:	3-spdM	3-spdM	3-spdM	3-spdM
Shift Location:	column	floor	column	column
Optional:	2-spdA	3-spdA	2-spdA	3-spdA
	3-spdA	4-spdM	3-spdA	3-spdM*
	4-spdM		3-spdM*	
			4-spdM	

Engine Option:	400/400 HO	Ram Air IV
Standard:	3-spdM*	4-spdM
Shift Location:	floor	floor
Optional:	3-spdA	3-spdA
	4-spdM	4-spdM

*Heavy-duty

Transmission Ratios

	3-spdM	4-spdM	2-spdA	3-spdA
first:	2.85	2.85	1.76	2.52
second:	1.68	2.02	1.00	1.52
third:	1.00	1.35	--	1.00
fourth:	--	1.00	--	--
reverse:	2.95	2.85	1.76	1.92

Rear Axle Ratios

Engine Hp:	175	215	265	325	330	335	345
Standard (M/T):	3.55	3.55	3.23	3.36	3.36(n)	3.36	3.90(n)
Standard (A/T):	3.23	3.23	2.56	3.23	3.08	3.08	3.90(n)
Optional:	3.08	2.78	2.78(c)	2.78(a,c)	3.23(a)	3.55(n)	
	3.28	3.55	2.93(a)	3.55(n)	3.55	3.90(n)	
				3.90	3.90(n)	4.33(n)	

a = with automatic; c = with air-conditioning; n = not with air-conditioning

EXTERIOR DATA

	hardtop	convertible
Overall Length (in):	191.1	191.1
Overall Width (in):	73.9	73.9
Overall Height (in):	49.6	49.5
Wheelbase (in):	108.1	108.1

Shipping Weight (lb):

base	3080	3330
350	3248	3498

EXTERIOR FINISHES

Color	Code	Color	Code
Starlight Black	A	Expresso Brown	B
Cameo White	C	Warwick Blue	D
Liberty Blue	E	Windward Blue	F
Antique Gold	G	Limelight Green	H
Crystal Turquoise	K	Midnight Green	M
Burgundy	N	Palladium Silver	P
Verdoro Green	Q	Matador Red	R
Champagne	S	Carousel Red	T
Goldenrod Yellow	W	Mayfair Maize	Y

UPHOLSTERY

Material	Color	Code	Material	Color	Code
Expanded Vinyl	Blue	00	Custom Int.		
	Gold	02	Knit Vinyl	Blue	10
	Green	06		Gold	12
	Parchment	07		Red	14
	Black	08		Green	16
				Parchment	17
				Black	18
				Parchment	27*
				Black	28*
* Hardtop only			Leather	Gold	93

Cordova Tops		Convertible Tops
Color	Code	Color
	1	White
Black	2	Black
Dark Blue	3	Dark Blue
Parchment	5	
Dark Fawn	8	
Dark Green	9	Dark Green

PRICE DATA

Base Price	hardtop	convertible
base	2831	3045
Sprint	2942	3156
350	2941	3155
HO	3017	3231
Ram Air	3663	3877
Trans Am	3556	3770

CURRENT VALUE (approximate)

Model Condition		Best	Very Good	Good	Fair	Poor
base	hardtop	5000	3500	2500	1500	750
	convertible	6200	4340	3100	1860	930
Sprint & 350 V-8	hardtop	5500	3850	2750	1650	825
	convertible	7700	5390	3850	2310	1155
400 HO	hardtop	5500	3850	2750	1650	825
	convertible	7700	5390	3850	2310	1155
Trans Am	hardtop	10500	7350	5250	3150	1575

*Add 15% for Ram Air; 30-50% for Ram Air II
Note: Since there were only a few convertible Trans Ams made, the going prices are extremely high.

POPULAR FACTORY OPTIONS

Item	Code	Price (nearest $)	
Air-conditioning	582	376	
Clock, Electric	474	16	
Console	472	54	
Cruise Control	441	58	(A/T&V-8 req.)
Differential	361	63	(std on T/A)
Engine, Ram Air IV	347	558	
			(400 only, 390 on T/A)
Glass, Tinted	531	33	
Glass, Tinted, windshield only	532	22	
Head Rests	571	17	
Instruments, Rally & Clock	484	47	
Instruments, Rally & Tach	444	84	
Mirror, remote control	424	11	
Power Brakes	502	42	
Power Brakes, Disc	511	64	
Power Seat, left bucket	564	74	
Power Steering	501	105	
Power Top	544	53	(conv.only)
Power Windows	551	105	
Ram Air Hood Inlet	611	84	
Radio, Pushbutton	382	61	
Radio, AM/FM	384	134	
Radio, AM/FM Stereo	388	239	
Rear Speaker	411	16	
Rear Window Defogger	404	22	
Seat Belts, custom front & rear	431	13	(37 on conv.)
Speedometer, Safeguard	442	16	
Steering Wheel, Sports	462	51	
Steering Wheel, tilt	504	45	
Tachometer, hood-mounted	471	63	

Tape, Stereo	412	134
Transmission, 3-spd manual floor	341	42
Transmission, 3-spd automatic	351	227
Transmission, 4-spd manual	358	195
Transmission, 2-spd automatic	352	174
Trunk Lid Remote Control	551	15
Vinyl Roof	–	90
Wheel Discs, deluxe	451	21
Wheel Discs, custom	452	41
Wheel Discs, wire	453	74
Wheels, Rally II	454	84

PERFORMANCE DATA

Source:	WORLD CAR	MOTOR TREND	ROAD TEST
Engine Hp:	175	265	345*
Transmission:	3-spdM	3-spdA	4-spdM
Rear Axle Ratio:	3.55	2.78	3.90
0 to 60 Time (secs):	nr	10.0	nr
1/4 Mile Time (secs):	nr	17.0	14.6
1/4 Mile Speed (mph):	nr	81	99.2
Maximum Speed (mph):	107	nr	nr
60 to 0 Braking Distance (ft):	nr	147	150.2
MPG (city):	nr	10.7	nr
MPG (highway):	nr	14.5	nr
MPG (combined):	nr	nr	11

* Trans Am
nr = not reported

Firebird Formula 400

Physical Features

In its first complete restyling job, Firebird took on an entirely new shape. It was a fastback coupe--no convertible or hardtop. The front end bore a strong resemblence to the contemporary GTO, but with single headlights instead of the GTO's dual lights. Instead of the various engine options, Firebird offered four different models. Each had its own standard engine, but each had one option as well. In the bargain basement was the base Firebird model powered by the Chevrolet six. Pontiac's overhead cam engine was no longer used. An optional engine in the base Firebird was the 350 V-8. It was also the standard engine in the Esprit model. The Esprit's optional engine was the 400 cid, 2-barrel V-8. Next up the Firebird ladder was the Formula 400. Its base engine was the 400 cid, 4-barrel V-8 and its option was the Ram Air III. The ultimate Firebird model was the Trans Am. It came with the Ram Air III, but Ram Air IV was optional. In addition to the chrome or painted logos indicating the model, there were certain features unique to the Formula 400 and Trans Am models. The former had air scoops near the front of the hood which protruded slightly. The Trans Am was fitted with air dams across the bottom of the front and in front of the wheels. There was a shaker hood and air extractors on the front fenders, as well as a spoiler on the rear deck.

Observations

Embarrassing delays caused a very late introduction of the 1970 Firebird. Production of the model was not much more than half that of the previous year. Sales, however, were down less than 5% during the calendar year thanks to the prolonged production of the 1969 models. Firebird's share of Pontiac sales during 1970 increased to over 10%. The Trans Am was now taking on the performance image for which it became famous. The air dams, spoiler, etc., said performance loud and clear and the engines confirmed it.

VIN NUMBERS

Vehicle Identification Number: 223( )0( )( )00001 and up
Explanation:
First symbol: GM division: Pontiac = 2
Second & third symbols: Series number: Firebird = 23
Fourth & fifth symbols: Body code:
    hardtop = 37
    convertible = 67
Sixth symbol: Last digit of model year
Seventh symbol: Letter indicating assembly plant
Eighth symbol: Number of cylinders:
    6 cyl = 6
    V-8 = 1
Ninth to thirteenth symbol: Sequential production number

PRODUCTION TOTALS

Model	M/T	%	A/T	%	Total	%
base	2899	5.9	15975	32.8	18874	38.7
Esprit	2104	4.3	16857	34.6	18961	38.9
Formula 400	2777	5.7	4931	10.1	7708	15.8
Trans Am	1798	3.7	1398	2.9	3196	6.6
Total	9578	19.6	36161	80.4	48739	100.0

Model	6 cyl	%	V-8	%
base	3134	16.6	15740	83.4

	Ram Air III	%	Ram Air IV	%
Trans Am & M/T	1769	55.4	29	0.9
Trans Am & A/T	1339	41.9	59	1.8
Total	3108	97.3	88	2.7

DRIVETRAIN DATA

base model, standard
Cylinder Configuration:	Inline
Number of Cylinders:	6
Cylinder Bore (in):	3.875
Cylinder Stroke (in):	3.53
Displacement (cu in):	249.8
Carburetion:	1 1-bbl
Carburetor Make:	Rochester
Carburetor Model:	MV
Compression Ratio:	8.5
Brake Horsepower:	155
RPM @ Maximum Hp:	4200
Torque, ft-lb:	235
RPM @ Maximum Torque:	1600

Esprit Option
Cylinder Configuration:	V
Number of Cylinders:	8
Cylinder Bore (in):	3.875
Cylinder Stroke (in):	3.75
Displacement (cu in):	353.8
Carburetion:	1 2-bbl
Carburetor Make:	Rochester
Carburetor Model:	2GV
Compression Ratio:	8.8
Brake Horsepower:	255
RPM @ Maximum Hp:	4600
Torque, ft-lb:	355
RPM @ Maximum Torque:	2800

Esprit Option

Cylinder Configuration:	V
Number of Cylinders:	8
Cylinder Bore (in):	4.12
Cylinder Stroke (in):	3.75
Displacement (cu in):	400.0
Carburetion:	1 2-bbl
Carburetor Make:	Rochester
Carburetor Model:	2GV
Compression Ratio:	8.8
Brake Horsepower:	265
RPM @ Maximum Hp:	4600
Torque, ft-lb:	397
RPM @ Maximum Torque:	2400

Trans Am standard

Cylinder Configuration:	V
Number of Cylinders:	8
Cylinder Bore (in):	4.12
Cylinder Stroke (in):	3.75
Displacement (cu in):	400.0
Carburetion:	1 4-bbl
Carburetor Make:	Rochester
Carburetor Model:	4MV
Compression Ratio:	10.5
Brake Horsepower:	345
RPM @ Maximum Hp:	5000
Torque, ft-lb:	430
RPM @ Maximum Torque:	3400

TRANSMISSIONS

Engine Hp:	155/255	265	330/345	Ram Air 345
Standard:	3-spdM	3-spdA	3-spdM	4-spdM
Shift Location:	column	floor*	floor	floor
Optional:	2-spdA		3-spdA	3-spdA
	3-spdA		4-spdM	
	4-spdM			

* If a center console was specified.

Transmission Ratios

	3-spdM	4-spdM	2-spdA	3-spdA
first:	2.85	2.52	1.76	2.52
second:	1.68	1.83	1.00	1.52
third:	1.00	1.48	--	1.00
fourth:	--	1.00	--	–
reverse:	2.85	2.85	1.76	1.92

Rear Axle Ratios

Engine Hp:	155	255	265	330	345	Ram Air 345
Standard (M/T):	3.08(n)	3.36(c)	--	3.55	3.55	3.55
Standard (A/T):	3.08	2.73	3.07	3.07	3.55	3.55
Optional:	3.08			3.31(a,c)	3.73(c)	3.73(c)
				3.73(c)		

a = with automatic; c = with air-conditioning;
n = not with air-conditioning

EXTERIOR DATA

Overall Length (in): 191.6
Overall Width (in): 73.4
Overall Height (in): 50.4
Wheelbase (in): 108.0
Shipping Weight (lb):

base	Esprit	Formula 400	Trans Am
3140	3435	3470	3550

EXTERIOR FINISHES

Color	Code	Color	Code
Palomino Copper	B	Polar White	C
Bermuda Blue	D	Atoll Blue	E
Lucerne Blue	F	Palisade Green	H
Castillian Bronze	J	Keylime Green	L
Palladium Silver	P	Verdoro Green	Q
Cardinal Red	R	Coronado Gold	S
Carousel Red	V	Goldenrod Yellow	W
Granada Gold	Z		

UPHOLSTERY

Material	Color	Code	Recommended Exterior Color
Vinyl	Blue	01	C,D,E,F,P
	Saddle	05	B,C,H,J,L,P,Q,R,S,V,Z
	Green	06	C,H,L,Q
	Sandalwood	07	any color
	Black	08	any color
Knit Vinyl*	Blue	11	C,D,E,F,P
	Brown	13	any color except V
	Red	14	C,R,V
	Saddle	15	B,C,H,J,L,P,Q,R,S,V,Z
	Green	16	C,H,L,Q
	Sandalwood	17	any color
	Black	18	any color
Cloth/Coated	Sandalwood	27	any color
Fabric*	Black	28	any color

*Custom trim

PRICE DATA

base	Esprit	Formula 400	Trans Am
2875	3241	3370	4305

CURRENT VALUE (approximate)

Model Condition	Best	Very Good	Good	Fair	Poor
base	4700	3290	2350	1410	705
Esprit	4800	3360	2400	1440	720
Formula 400	9000	6300	4500	2700	1350
Trans Am	11000	7700	5500	3300	1650

*Add for Ram Air

POPULAR FACTORY OPTIONS

Item	Code	Price (nearest $)	
Air-conditioning	582	376	
Clock, Electric	492	16	
Console	494	59	
Cordova Top	SVT	90	
Deck Lid Release	554	15	
Differential, Safe-T-Track	361	42	
Engine, 350 cid	L30	111	(base model only)
Engine, Ram Air III	L74	169	(Formula 400 only)
Engine, Ram Air IV	347	390	(Trans Am only)
Glass, Tinted	531	33	
Glass, Tinted, windshield only	532	26	
Instruments, Rally & Clock	488	47	
Instruments, Rally & Hood Tach	484	95	
Mirrors, 2, left remote control	434	26	
Power Brakes	502	42	
Power Door Locks	734	45	
Power Steering	501	105	
Power Windows	551	105	
Radio, Pushbutton	382	61	
Radio, AM/FM	384	134	
Radio, AM/FM Stereo	388	239	
Rear Speaker	411	16	
Rear Window Defogger	541	26	

Seat Belts, custom front & rear	431	39
Steering Wheel, Deluxe	461	16
Steering Wheel, Formula	464	42
Steering Wheel, tilt	504	45
Tachometer, hood-mounted	491	63
Tape, Stereo	412	134
Transmission, 3-spd manual floor	M13	84
Transmission, 3-spd automatic	M40	227
Transmission, 4-spd manual	M21	195
Wheel Covers, wire	473	74
Wheels, Rally II	474	84

PERFORMANCE DATA

Source:	CAR & DRIVER	CAR & DRIVER	CAR & DRIVER
Model:	Esprit	Formula 400	Trans Am
Engine Hp:	255	330	345
Transmission:	3-spdA	3-spdA	4-spdM
Rear Axle Ratio:	2.73	3.07	3.73
0 to 60 Time (sec):	9.8	6.4	5.7
1/4 Mile Time (sec):	17.2	14.7	14.1
1/4 Mile Speed (mph):	79.4	98.9	103.2
Maximum Speed (mph):	nr	nr	nr
80 to 0 Braking Distance (ft):	248	292	255
MPG (city):	nr	nr	nr
MPG (highway):	nr	nr	nr
MPG (combined):	nr	nr	nr

nr = not reported

1971

Physical Features

Very little in the way of appearance changes were made to the 1971 Firebird after its short year with the new body. All models except the Trans Am got louvered front fenders, but that was about it. Virtually the same models were available. Modifications were made to some engines because of stricter exhaust emission standards imposed by the Federal Government. In other cases, different engines were used. Power was down in the six and the 350 V-8. The two-barrel 400 retained its power rating, while the four-barrel version suffered some power loss. [All engines appeared to suffer more than they actually did due to the change from quoting gross ratings to quoting net ratings.] Ram Air III and IV were no longer used and Pontiac's 455 cubic inch engine became Firebird's highest performance motor. the 455 4-barrel was standard in the Formula. The 455 HO version was standard in Trans Am and optional in the Formula. With that engine, it became known as the Formula 455. Otherwise, the Formula 400 name continued. The Trans Am, as usual, was easily identified by its white-with-blue trim with a few finished in the reverse combination.

Observations

The ponycar market was in a prolonged slump. The Firebird ended calendar 1971 with a drop of nearly 7% in registrations. That was not as great a drop, however, as the other ponycars sustained. Firebird fell to almost 8% of total Pontiac sales but that was mainly because of improvements in the sale of other Pontiac lines. Production of the Trans Am tumbled by one-third. Still, it was establishing a solid reputation.

Trans Am

VIN NUMBERS

Vehicle Identification Number: 223( )1( )( )00001 and up
Explanation:
First symbol: GM division: Pontiac = 2
Second & third symbols: Series number: Firebird = 23
Fourth & fifth symbols: Body code: coupe = 87
Sixth symbol: Last digit of model year
Seventh symbol: Letter indicating assembly plant
Eighth symbol: Number of cylinders:
    6 cyl = 6
    V-8 = 1
Ninth to thirteenth symbol: Sequential production number

PRODUCTION TOTALS

Model	M/T	%	A/T	%	Total	%
base	2778	5.2	20244	38.1	23022	43.3
Esprit	947	1.8	19238	36.2	20185	38.0
Formula 400	1860	3.5	5942	11.2	7802	14.7
Trans Am	885	1.7	1231	2.3	2116	4.0
Total	6470	12.2	46655	87.8	53125	100.0

Model	6 cyl	%	V-8	%
base	2975	12.9	20047	87.1

DRIVETRAIN DATA

base model, standard

Cylinder Configuration:	Inline
Number of Cylinders:	6
Cylinder Bore (in):	3.875
Cylinder Stroke (in):	3.53
Displacement (cu in):	249.8
Carburetion:	1 1-bbl
Carburetor Make:	Rochester
Carburetor Model:	MV
Compression Ratio:	8.5
Brake Horsepower:	145
RPM @ Maximum Hp:	4200
Torque, ft-lb:	230
RPM @ Maximum Torque:	1600

Esprit standard & Formula

Cylinder Configuration:	V
Number of Cylinders:	8
Cylinder Bore (in):	3.875
Cylinder Stroke (in):	3.75
Displacement (cu in):	353.8
Carburetion:	1 2-bbl
Carburetor Make:	Rochester
Carburetor Model:	2GV
Compression Ratio:	8.0
Brake Horsepower:	250
RPM @ Maximum Hp:	4400
Torque, ft-lb:	350
RPM @ Maximum Torque:	2400

Esprit Option
Cylinder Configuration: V
Number of Cylinders: 8
Cylinder Bore (in):   4.12
Cylinder Stroke (in):   3.75
Displacement (cu in):   400.0
Carburetion: 1 2-bbl
Carburetor Make: Rochester
Carburetor Model: 2GV
Compression Ratio: 8.2
Brake Horsepower: 265
RPM @ Maximum Hp: 4400
Torque, ft-lb: 400
RPM @ Maximum Torque: 3600

Formula 400 standard
Cylinder Configuration: V
Number of Cylinders: 8
Cylinder Bore (in):   4.12
Cylinder Stroke (in):   3.75
Displacement (cu in):   400.0
Carburetion: 1 4-bbl
Carburetor Make: Rochester
Carburetor Model: 4MV
Compression Ratio: 8.2
Brake Horsepower: 300
RPM @ Maximum Hp: 4800
Torque, ft-lb: 400
RPM @ Maximum Torque: 3600

Formula 455 standard		Trans Am standard	
Cylinder Configuration:	V	Formula 455 Option	
Number of Cylinders:	8	Cylinder Configuration:	V
Cylinder Bore (in):	4.15	Number of Cylinders:	8
Cylinder Stroke (in):	4.21	Cylinder Bore (in):	4.15
Displacement (cu in):	455.6	Cylinder Stroke (in):	4.21
Carburetion:	1 4-bbl	Displacement (cu in):	455.6
Carburetor Make:	Rochester	Carburetion:	1 4-bbl
Carburetor Model:	4MV	Carburetor Make:	Rochester
Compression Ratio:	8.2	Carburetor Model:	4MV
Brake Horsepower:	325	Compression Ratio:	8.4
RPM @ Maximum Hp:	4400	Brake Horsepower:	335
Torque, ft-lb:	455	RPM @ Maximum Hp:	4800
RPM @ Maximum Torque:	3200	Torque, ft-lb:	480
		RPM @ Maximum Torque:	3600

TRANSMISSIONS

Engine Hp:	**145/250**	**300**	**325**	**335**
Standard:	3-spdM	3-spdM	3-spdA	4-spdM
Shift Location:	column	floor	floor*	floor
Optional:	2-spdA	4-spdM		3-spdM
	3-spdA	3-spdA		3-spdA
	4-spdM			

*If center console was specified.

Transmission Ratios

	3-spdM	4-spdM	2-spdA	3-spdA
first:	2.85	2.52	1.76	2.52
second:	1.68	1.83	1.00	1.52
third:	1.00	1.48	--	1.00
fourth:	--	1.00	--	–
reverse:	2.95	2.85	1.76	1.92

Rear Axle Ratios

Engine Hp:	145	250	300	325	335
Standard (M/T):	3.08(n)	3.42	3.42	--	3.42
Standard (A/T):	3.08(n)	2.73	3.08	3.42	3.42
Optional:		3.08(a)	3.73(n)	3.08(c)	3.08(c)
					3.42(n)

a = with automatic; c = with air-conditioning;
n = not with air-conditioning

EXTERIOR DATA

Overall Length (in):	191.6
Overall Width (in):	73.4
Overall Height (in):	50.4
Wheelbase (in):	108.0

Shipping Weight (lb):

base	Esprit	Formula 400	Trans Am
3164	3423	3473	3578

EXTERIOR FINISHES

Color	Code	Color	Code
Starlight Black	A	Sandalwood	B
Cameo White	C	Adriatic Blue	D
Regency Blue	E	Lucerne Blue	F
Limekist Green	H	Tropical Lime	L
Laurential Green	M	Rosewood	N
Nordic Silver	P	Cardinal Red	R
Castillian Bronze	S	Canyon Copper	T
Bronzini Gold	W	Quetzal Gold	Y
Aztec Gold	Z		

Note: Most Trans Ams were Cameo White and
the rest were Lucerne Blue

UPHOLSTERY

Style	Color	Code	Recommended Exterior Colors
standard	Blue	201	A,C,D,F,P
	Saddle	203	A,B,C,D,H,L,M,N,P,R,S,T,Y,Z
	Jade	206	A,B,C,H,L,M,Y,Z
	Sandalwood	207	A,B,C,H,L,M,N,P,R,S,T,Y,Z
	Black	209	any color
Custom	Blue	211	A,C,D,F,P
	Ivory	212	any color
	Saddle	213	A,B,C,D,H,L,M,N,P,R,S,T,Y,Z
	Sienna	214	A,B,C,H,S,T,Y,Z
	Jade	216	A,B,C,H,L,M,Y,Z
	Sandalwood	217	A,B,C,H,L,M,N,P,R,S,T,Y,Z
	Black	219	any color

PRICE DATA

base	Esprit	Formula 400	Trans Am
3047	3416	3446	4595

CURRENT VALUE (approximate)

Model Condition	Best	Very Good	Good	Fair	Poor
base	4500	3150	2250	1350	675
Esprit	4800	3360	2400	1440	720
Formula 400	8500	5950	4250	2550	1275
Trans Am	10000	7000	5000	3000	1500

POPULAR FACTORY OPTIONS

Item	Code	Price (nearest $)	
Air-conditioning	582	402	
Bumper Guards	734	16	
Clock, Electric	722	16	
Console	431	61	
Console, rear	422	26	
Differential, Safe-T-Track	361	44	
Differential, Safe-T-Track HD	368	67	
Engine, 250 hp	L30	121	(base model only)
Engine, 265 hp	L65	53	(Esprit only)
Engine, 300 hp	L78	100	
Engine, 325 hp	L75	158	
Engine, 335 hp	LS5	237	(Formula only)
Glass, Tinted	531	38	
Glass, Tinted, windshield only	532	31	
Hood Air Inlet	601	84	(Formula only)
Instruments, Rally & Clock	718	47	
Instruments, Rally & Hood Tach	714	95	
Mirrors, 2, left remote control	434	26	
Power Brakes	502	47	
Power Door Locks	554	45	
Power Steering	501	111	
Power Windows	551	115	
Radio, Pushbutton	401	66	
Radio, AM/FM	403	139	
Radio, AM/FM Stereo	405	239	
Rear Speaker	411	19	
Rear Air Spoiler	572	33	(Formula only)
Rear Window Defogger	541	32	
Rear Window Defroster	534	63	
Seat Belts, custom front & rear	451	16	
Spare Tire, Space-Saver	684	16	
Steering Wheel, Formula	464	42	(58 on base)
Steering Wheel, tilt	504	45	(P/S req.)

Tape, Stereo (8-track)	412	134	
Tape, Stereo (cassette)	414	134	
Transmission, 3-spd manual floor	M13	84	
Transmission, 3-spd automatic	M38	211	(222 w/V-8)
Transmission, 4-spd manual	M20	206	
Transmission, 2-spd automatic	M35	180	(190 w/V-8)
Trunk Lid Remote Control	421	15	
Wheel Discs, custom	472	32	
Wheel Discs, wire	473	84	(58 on Esprit)
Wheels, Honeycomb	478	37	(100 on Esprit)
Wheels, Rally II	474	90	(63 on Esprit)

PERFORMANCE DATA

Source:	WORLD CAR	WORLD CAR	WORLD CAR
Engine Hp:	300	325	335
Transmission:	3-spdM	3-spdA	3-spdM
Rear Axle Ratio:	3.42	3.42	3.42
0 to 60 Time (sec):	nr	nr	nr
1/4 Mile Time (sec):	nr	nr	nr
1/4 Mile Speed (mph):	nr	nr	nr
Maximum Speed (mph):	115	120	122
80 to 0 Braking Distance (ft):	nr	nr	nr
MPG (city):	nr	nr	nr
MPG (highway):	nr	nr	nr
MPG (combined):	12.6	12.2	11.9

nr = not reported

Physical Features

Very slight modifications were made to the grille of the 1972 Firebirds. The mesh was changed from the squared pattern of the 1971 models to an elongated honeycomb design. Little else about the external appearance was different. Engines were changed, mainly because of government imposed pollution regulations. The same basic engines were continued in the same models as in the previous year.

Observations

While the ponycar market continued its downward tumble, Firebird sales also fell. For calendar 1972, there were 60% fewer Firebird sales than the year before. Part of this was due to a long strike at the Lordstown, Ohio plant where Firebirds and Camaros were built, but much was due to a general deterioration in the ponycar market. If there was any reason for Pontiac to find cheer in this, it was the fact that Camaro sales suffered even worse than this those of the Firebird. However, what comfort there may have been in that was more than offset by the grim fact that Firebird accounted for a fraction over 3% of total Pontiac sales for the year. The disasterous Firebird sales in calendar 1972 were reflected proportionally in Trans Am production during the model year. This was the bottom for the Firebird. There was no place to go but up and it was about to soar to great heights.

Firebird Formula 400

58

VIN NUMBERS

Vehicle Identification Number: 2( )87( )( )2( )500001 and up
Explanation:
First symbol: GM division: Pontiac = 2
Second symbol: Series number:
    base Firebird = S
    Esprit = T
    Formula = U
    Trans Am = V
Third & fourth symbols: Body code: coupe = 87
Fifth symbol: Letter indicating engine:
    D = 110 hp
    M = 160 hp
    R = 175 hp
    T = 250 hp
    X = 300 hp
Sixth symbol: Last digit of model year
Seventh symbol: Letter indicating assembly plant
Eighth to thirteenth symbol:
    Sequential production number starting with 500001

PRODUCTION TOTALS

Model	M/T	%	A/T	%	Total	%
base	1263	4.2	10738	35.8	12001	40.1
Esprit	504	1.7	10911	36.4	11415	38.1
Formula	1082	3.6	4167	13.9	5249	17.5
Trans Am	458	1.5	828	2.8	1286	4.3
Total	3307	11.0	26644	88.9	29951	100.0#

May not total 100 due to rounding

DRIVETRAIN DATA

base model, standard	D
Cylinder Configuration:	Inline
Number of Cylinders:	6
Cylinder Bore (in):	3.875
Cylinder Stroke (in):	3.53
Displacement (cu in):	249.8
Carburetion:	1 1-bbl
Carburetor Make:	Rochester
Carburetor Model:	MV
Compression Ratio:	8.5
Brake Horsepower:	110
RPM @ Maximum Hp:	3800
Torque, ft-lb:	140
RPM @ Maximum Torque:	3600

Esprit standard:	H	Formula standard:	H
Cylinder Configuration:	V	Cylinder Configuration:	V
Number of Cylinders:	8	Number of Cylinders:	8
Cylinder Bore (in):	3.875	Cylinder Bore (in):	3.875
Cylinder Stroke (in):	3.75	Cylinder Stroke (in):	3.75
Displacement (cu in):	353.8	Displacement (cu in):	353.8
Carburetion:	1 2-bbl	Carburetion:	2-bbl
Carburetor Make:	Rochester	Carburetor Make:	Rochester
Carburetor Model:	2GV	Carburetor Model:	2GV
Compression Ratio:	8.0	Compression Ratio:	8.0
Brake Horsepower:	160	Brake Horsepower:	175
RPM @ Maximum Hp:	4400	RPM @ Maximum Hp:	4400
Torque, ft-lb:	270	Torque, ft-lb:	270
RPM @ Maximum Torque:	2000	RPM @ Maximum Torque:	2000

Esprit Option:	R
Cylinder Configuration:	V
Number of Cylinders:	8
Cylinder Bore (in):	4.12
Cylinder Stroke (in):	3.75
Displacement (cu in):	400.0
Carburetion:	1 2-bbl
Carburetor Make:	Rochester
Carburetor Model:	2GV
Compression Ratio:	8.2
Brake Horsepower:	175
RPM @ Maximum Hp:	4400
Torque, ft-lb:	310
RPM @ Maximum Torque:	2400

Formula 400 standard:	S
Cylinder Configuration:	V
Number of Cylinders:	8
Cylinder Bore (in):	4.12
Cylinder Stroke (in):	3.75
Displacement (cu in):	400.0
Carburetion:	1 4-bbl
Carburetor Make:	Rochester
Carburetor Model:	4MV
Compression Ratio:	8.2
Brake Horsepower:	250
RPM @ Maximum Hp:	4400
Torque, ft-lb:	325
RPM @ Maximum Torque:	3200

Trans Am standard:	X	Formula Option:	X
Cylinder Configuration:	V	Cylinder Configuration:	V
Number of Cylinders:	8	Number of Cylinders:	8
Cylinder Bore (in):	4.15	Cylinder Bore (in):	4.15
Cylinder Stroke (in):	4.21	Cylinder Stroke (in):	4.21
Displacement (cu in):	455.6	Displacement (cu in):	455.6
Carburetion:	1 4-bbl	Carburetion:	1 4-bbl

Carburetor Make:	Rochester	Carburetor Make:	Rochester
Carburetor Model:	4MV	Carburetor Model:	4MV
Compression Ratio:	8.4	Compression Ratio:	8.4
Brake Horsepower:	300	Brake Horsepower:	300
RPM @ Maximum Hp:	4000	RPM @ Maximum Hp:	4000
Torque, ft-lb:	415	Torque, ft-lb:	415
RPM @ Maximum Torque:	3200	RPM @ Maximum Torque:	3200

TRANSMISSIONS

Engine Hp:	110	160	175	200	300
Standard:	3-spdM	3-spdM	3-spdA	4-spdM	4-spdM
Shift Location:	column	floor	floor*	floor	floor
Optional:	2-spdA	4-spdM		3-spdM	3-spdA
	3-spdA	2-spdA		3-spdA	

*If center console was specified

Transmission Ratios

	3-spdM	4-spdM	2-spdA	3-spdA
first:	2.85	2.52	1.82	2.48
second:	1.68	1.83	1.00	1.48
third:	1.00	1.48	--	1.00
fourth:	--	1.00	--	--
reverse:	2.95	2.59	1.82	2.08

Rear Axle Ratios

Engine Hp:	110	160	175	200	300
Standard (M/T):	3.08(n)	3.42	3.42	--	3.42
Standard (A/T):	3.08(n)	2.73	2.73	2.73	3.08
Optional:		3.08	3.08	3.08	3.42(a)

a = with automatic; n = not with air-conditioning

EXTERIOR DATA

Overall Length (in): 191.6
Overall Width (in): 73.4
Overall Height (in): 50.4
Wheelbase (in): 108.0
Shipping Weight (lb):

base	Formula 350	Esprit	Formula 400	Trans Am
3169	3221	3357	3424	3564

EXTERIOR FINISHES

Color	Code	Color	Code
Starlight Black	A	Cameo White	C
Adriatic Blue	D	Quetzal Gold	E
Lucerne Blue	F	Brittany Beige	G
Shadow Gold	H	Brasilia Gold	J
Julep Green	K	Springfield Green	L
Wilderness Green	M	Revere Silver	N
Antique Pewter	P	Cardinal Red	R
Anaconda Gold	S	Cinnamon Bronze	T
Cumberland Blue	U	Spice Beige	V
Arizona Gold	W	Monarch Yellow	Y
Sundance Orange	Z		

Note: Most Trans Ams were Cameo White and
the rest were Lucerne Blue

UPHOLSTERY

Material	Color	Code
Morrokide	Ivory	121
	Saddle	131
	Green	141
	Black	161
	Blue	211
	Ivory	221
	Saddle	231
	Green	241
	Beige	251
	Black	261
Cloth/Morrokide	Beige	351
	Black	361

PRICE DATA

base	Esprit	Formula 350	Formula 400	Formula 455	Trans Am
2838	3194	3221	3318	3452	4256

CURRENT VALUE (approximate)

Model Condition	Best	Very Good	Good	Fair	Poor
base	4000	2800	2000	1200	600
Esprit	4400	3080	2200	1320	660
Formula	7800	5460	3900	2340	1170
Trans Am	9000	6300	4500	2700	1350

POPULAR FACTORY OPTIONS

Item	Code	Price (nearest $)
Air-conditioning	582	408
Bumper Guards	732	16
Clock, Electric	722	16

Console	431	59	
Console. rear	424	26	
Differential, Safe-T-Track	361	46	
Glass, Tinted	531	38	
Glass, Tinted, windshield only	532	31	
Instruments, Rally & Clock	718	47	
Instruments, Rally, Clock, Tach	714	95	
Mirrors, 2, left remote control	434	26	
Power Brakes	502	47	
Power Door Locks	554	45	
Power Steering	501	116	
Power Windows	551	116	(Console req.)
Radio, Pushbutton	401	66	
Radio, AM/FM	403	139	
Radio, AM/FM Stereo	405	239	
Rear Speaker	411	19	
Rear Window Defogger	541	32	
Rear Window Defroster	534	63	
Seat Belts, custom front & rear	451	16	
Spare Tire, Space-Saver	684	16	
Steering Wheel, tilt	504	44	(P/S req.)
Tape, 8-track	412	134	
Transmission, 3-spd manual floor	M12	11	
Transmission, 3-spd automatic	M38	211	(243 w/400 & 455)
Transmission, 4-spd manual	M20	206	(238 w/HO)
Transmission, 2-spd automatic	M35	180	(190 w/V-8)
Wheel Discs, deluxe	476	32	
Wheels, Honeycomb	478	126	(100 on Esprit)
Wheels, Rally II	474	90	(63 on Esprit)

PERFORMANCE DATA

Source:	WORLD CAR	WORLD CAR	WORLD CAR
Engine Hp:	160	175	300
Transmission:	3-spdM	3-spdA	3-spdM
Rear Axle Ratio:	3.42	2.73	3.42
0 to 60 Time (sec):	nr	nr	nr
1/4 Mile Time (sec):	nr	nr	nr
1/4 Mile Speed (mph):	nr	nr	nr
Maximum Speed (mph):	110	113	120
80 to 0 Braking Distance (ft):	nr	nr	nr
MPG (city):	nr	nr	nr
MPG (highway):	nr	nr	nr
MPG (combined):	14.3	14.1	11.8

nr = not reported

Physical Features

A rectangular pattern mesh in the grille cavities was the most extensive exterior change made to the Firebirds for 1973. The greatest variety of engines was now available and the Formula offered the widest choice. The Formula 350 engine was the Esprit option. The Formula 400 used the 400 cid V-8. The Formula 455 could be ordered with either the basic 455 or the SD 455 V-8 which were also used in the Trans Am. The Trans Am was no longer offered in blue, but dark green, red and white. One of the most popular options on the Trans Am was the huge $55 hood decal of the firebird, or "screaming chicken" as it has been dubbed.

Observations

Firebird's fortunes had turned the corner and were on the way to great success. Sales suddenly jumped 132% to over 50,000 cars. The Trans Am segment of the Firebird range was beginning to catch fire. Just over 4,800 were built during the model year. Although that was a record, it was a fragile one, soon to be shattered and quickly forgotten.

Firebird

VIN NUMBERS

Vehicle Identification Number: 2( )87( )( )3( )100001 and up
Explanation:
First symbol: GM division: Pontiac = 2
Second symbol: Series number:
    base Firebird = S
    Esprit = T
    Formula = U
    Trans Am = V
Third & fourth symbols: Body code: coupe = 87
Fifth symbol: Letter indicating engine:
    D = 100 hp
    M = 150 hp
    R = 170 hp
    T = 250 hp
    X = 310 hp
Sixth symbol: Last digit of model year
Seventh symbol: Letter indicating assembly plant
Eighth to thirteenth symbol:
    Sequential production number starting with 100001

PRODUCTION TOTALS

Model	M/T	%	A/T	%	Total	%
base	1370	3.0	12726	27.5	14096	30.4
Esprit	–	--	17249	37.2	17249	37.2
Formula	–	--	10166	22.0	10166	22.0
Trans Am	–	--	4802	10.4	4802	10.4
Total	1370	3.0	44943	97.1	46313	100.0

SD 455 Engines   Formula   43
                  Trans Am 252   (180 3-spdA; 72 4-spdM)

Transmission Installations

	Units	Percent
3-spdM	2145	4.6
4-spdM	4237	9.2
3-spdM	39931	86.2
Total	46313	100.0

DRIVETRAIN DATA

base model, standard:	D*
Cylinder Configuration:	Inline
Number of Cylinders:	6
Cylinder Bore (in):	3.875
Cylinder Stroke (in):	3.53
Displacement (cu in):	249.8
Carburetion:	1 1-bbl
Carburetor Make:	Rochester
Carburetor Model:	MV
Compression Ratio:	8.25
Brake Horsepower:	100
RPM @ Maximum Hp:	3600
Torque, ft-lb:	175
RPM @ Maximum Torque:	1600

*not available with air-conditioning

Esprit standard:	M	Formula standard:	M
Cylinder Configuration:	V	Cylinder Configuration:	V
Number of Cylinders:	8	Number of Cylinders:	8
Cylinder Bore (in):	3.875	Cylinder Bore (in):	3.875
Cylinder Stroke (in):	3.75	Cylinder Stroke (in):	3.75
Displacement (cu in):	353.8	Displacement (cu in):	353.8
Carburetion:	1 2-bbl	Carburetion:	1 2-bbl
Carburetor Make:	Rochester	Carburetor Make:	Rochester
Carburetor Model:	2GV	Carburetor Model:	2GV
Compression Ratio:	7.6	Compression Ratio:	7.6
Brake Horsepower:	150	Brake Horsepower:	175

RPM @ Maximum Hp:	4000	RPM @ Maximum Hp:	4000
Torque, ft-lb:	270	Torque, ft-lb:	270
RPM @ Maximum Torque:	2000	RPM @ Maximum Torque:	2000

Esprit Option:	R
Cylinder Configuration:	V
Number of Cylinders:	8
Cylinder Bore (in):	4.12
Cylinder Stroke (in):	3.75
Displacement (cu in):	400.0
Carburetion:	1 2-bbl
Carburetor Make:	Rochester
Carburetor Model:	2GV
Compression Ratio:	8.0
Brake Horsepower:	170
RPM @ Maximum Hp:	3600
Torque, ft-lb:	320
RPM @ Maximum Torque:	2000

Formula 400:	S
Cylinder Configuration:	V
Number of Cylinders:	8
Cylinder Bore (in):	4.12
Cylinder Stroke (in):	3.75
Displacement (cu in):	400.0
Carburetion:	1 4-bbl
Carburetor Make:	Rochester
Carburetor Model:	4MV
Compression Ratio:	8.0
Brake Horsepower:	230 (200 w/M/T)
RPM @ Maximum Hp:	4400 (4000 w/M/T)
Torque, ft-lb:	325 (310 w/M/T)
RPM @ Maximum Torque:	3200 (2400 w/M/T)

Trans Am standard:	W
Cylinder Configuration:	V
Number of Cylinders:	8
Cylinder Bore (in):	4.151
Cylinder Stroke (in):	4.206
Displacement (cu in):	455.4
Carburetion:	1 4-bbl
Carburetor Make:	Rochester
Carburetor Model:	4MV
Compression Ratio:	8.0
Brake Horsepower:	250
RPM @ Maximum Hp:	4000
Torque, ft-lb:	370
RPM @ Maximum Torque:	2800

Trans Am option:	X	Formula option:	X
Cylinder Configuration:	V	Cylinder Configuration:	V
Number of Cylinders:	8	Number of Cylinders:	8
Cylinder Bore (in):	4.151	Cylinder Bore (in):	4.151
Cylinder Stroke (in):	4.206	Cylinder Stroke (in):	4.206
Displacement (cu in):	455.4	Displacement (cu in):	455.4
Carburetion:	1 4-bbl	Carburetion:	1 4-bbl
Carburetor Make:	Rochester	Carburetor Make:	Rochester
Carburetor Model:	4MV	Carburetor Model:	4MV
Compression Ratio:	8.4	Compression Ratio:	8.4
Brake Horsepower:	310	Brake Horsepower:	310
RPM @ Maximum Hp:	4000	RPM @ Maximum Hp:	4000
Torque, ft-lb:	390	Torque, ft-lb:	390
RPM @ Maximum Torque:	3600	RPM @ Maximum Torque:	3600

TRANSMISSIONS

Engine Hp:	100	150	170	200	250	300
Standard:	3-spdM	3-spdM	3-spdM	3-spdA	4-spdM	4-spdM
Optional:	3-spdA	4-spdM	4-spdM	4-spdM*	3-spdA	3-spdA
		3-spdA	3-spdA			

*230 hp

Transmission Ratios

	3-spdM		4-spdM		3-spdA	
first:	2.85	2.54#	2.20	2.52	2.52	2.44+
second:	1.68	1.50#	1.64	1.88	1.52	1.48+
third:	1.00	1.00#	1.28	1.46	1.00	1.00+
fourth:	--	--	1.00	1.00	--	--
reverse:	2.95	2.63#	2.27	2.35	1.92	2.08+

350 cid; + 400/455 cid

Rear Axle Ratios

Engine Hp:	100	150	170	200	250	310
Standard (M/T):	3.08	3.08	--	3.42	3.42	3.42
Standard (A/T):	3.08	2.73	2.73	3.08	3.08	3.42
Optional:		3.08(a)	3.08	3.42	3.42	
		3.42				

a = with automatic

EXTERIOR DATA

Overall Length (in):   192.1
Overall Width (in):   73.4
Overall Height (in):   50.4
Wheelbase (in):   108.0
Shipping Weight (lb):

base	Esprit	Formula	Trans Am
3159	3309	3318	3504

EXTERIOR FINISHES

Color	Code	Color	Code
Starlight Black	A	Cameo White	C
Porcelain Blue	D	Admiralty Blue	E
Regatta Blue	F	Mesa Tan	G
Desert Sand	H	Golden Olive	J
Verdent Green	K	Slate Green	L
Brewster Green	M	Buccaneer Red	R
Florentine Red	S	Sunlight Yellow	T
Navajo Orange	U	Ascot Silver	V
Burnished Umber	W	Valencia Gold	Y
Burma Brown	Z		

NOTE: Trans Am colors were Cameo White,
Brewster Green or Bucccaneer Red only

UPHOLSTERY

Material	Color	Code	Recommended Exterior Colors
Morrokide	White	321	C,D,E,F,H,J,K,L,M,R,S,T,U,V,Y,Z
	Saddle	331	C,H,J,L,M,T,U,V,Y,Z
	Black	361	C,D,E,F,H,J,K,L,M,R,S,T,U,V,Y,Z
	White	421*	C,D,E,F,H,J,K,L,M,R,S,T,U,V,Y,Z
	Saddle	431*	C,H,J,L,M,T,U,V,Y,Z
	Black	461*	C,D,E,F,H,J,K,L,M,R,S,T,U,V,Y,Z
	Burgundy	471*	C,E,S
Cloth/ Morrokide	Beige	551*	C,E,H,J,K,L,M,R,S,T,U,V,Y,Z

*Custom Interiors, extra cost on Formula and Trans Am

PRICE DATA

base	Esprit	Formula 350	Formula 400	Formula 455	Trans Am
2838	2956	3221	3318	3896	4256

CURRENT VALUE (approximate)

Model Condition	Best	Very Good	Good	Fair	Poor
base	3500	2450	1750	1050	525
Esprit	3900	2730	1950	1170	585
Formula	8600	6020	4300	2580	1290
Trans Am	11500	8050	5750	3450	1725

POPULAR FACTORY OPTIONS

Item	Code	Price (nearest $)	
Air-conditioning	582	397	
Bumper Guards, rear	732	15	
Clock, Electric	711	15	
Console	431	57	
Differential, Safe-T-Track	371	45	
Engine, SD 455	LS2	521	(675 on Formula)
Glass, Tinted	531	37	
Glass, Tinted, windshield only	532	30	
Hood Decal	512	55	(Trans Am only)
Instruments, Rally & Clock	712	46	
Instruments, Rally, Clock & Tach	714	92	
Mirrors, 2, left remote control	434	26	
Power Brakes, Disc	502	46	
Power Door Locks	654	44	
Power Steering	501	113	
Power Windows	551	75	(Console req.)
Radio, Pushbutton	411	65	
Radio, AM/FM	413	135	
Radio, AM/FM Stereo	415	233	
Rear Speaker	421	18	
Rear Window Defogger	541	31	
Rear Window Defroster	534	62	

Seat Belts, custom front & rear	451	15	
Spare Tire, Space-Saver	684	15	
Steering Wheel, tilt	504	41	
Tape, 8-track	422	130	
Transmission, 3-spd automatic	M38	205	(215 w/350; 236 w/400&455)
Transmission, 4-spd manual	M20	200	
Wheel Discs, custom finned	472	50	(24 on Esprit)
Wheels, Honeycomb	478	123	(97 on Esprit)
Wheels, Rally II	474	87	

PERFORMANCE DATA

Source:	ROAD TEST	WORLD CAR	CAR & DRIVER
Engine Hp:	170	250	310
Rear Axle Ratio:	3.08	3.42	3.42
0 to 60 Time (sec):	11.2	nr	5.4
1/4 Mile Time (sec):	17.1	nr	13.8
1/4 Mile Speed (mph):	86	nr	103.6
Maximum Speed (mph):	112	119	132
60 to 0 Braking Distance (ft):	167	nr	226*
MPG (city):	14.0	nr	nr
MPG (highway):	16.2	nr	nr
MPG (combined):	nr	12.6	10-13

nr = not reported
*from 70 mph

Physical Features

After several years of very minor appearance changes, the front end of the Firebird was redesigned. It was quite sloped and the grille consisted of two rectangles. Fine vertical bars in these cavities made up the grillework. More engine modifications were aimed at reducing exhaust emissions in accordance with Federal law. There were some reductions in power ratings. Basically the same engines were offered, however, and made available in the same models as in 1974. For the performance-minded, the SD 455, down a bit in horsepower, was obtainable in the Formula or Trans Am.

Observations

The sudden upsurge in Firebird sales during 1973 was no temporary phenomenon. Sales soared again in 1974, scoring a 29% increase. This model reached a new high of almost 13% of Pontiac sales. Production rose to meet the higher demands and climbed to more than 73,700. Perhaps the greatest surprise in the Firebird's popularity was the 114% increase in Trans Am production. That was more than the number of Formulas made the year before. Even Formula production for 1974 more than doubled. The increased popularity of these higher powered Firebirds is amazing. This was during the energy crisis when most people forgot performance and were falling over themselves trying to get cars that were much more fuel-efficient. In the face of that panic, Firebird was bucking the trend.

Trans Am SD-455

VIN NUMBERS

Vehicle Identification Number: 2( )87( )( )4( )100001 and up
Explanation:
First symbol: GM division: Pontiac = 2
Second symbol: Series number:
base Firebird = S
   Esprit = T
   Formula = U
   Trans Am = V
Third & fourth symbols: Body code: coupe = 87
Fifth symbol: Letter indicating engine:
   D = 100 hp
   M = 155 hp
   R = 175 hp
   T = 225 hp
   Y = 250 hp
   X = 290 hp
Sixth symbol: Last digit of model year
Seventh symbol: Letter indicating assembly plant
Eighth to thirteenth symbols:
   Sequential production number starting with 100001

PRODUCTION TOTALS

Model	6 cyl	%	V-8	%	Total	%
base	7603	10.3	18769	25.5	26372	35.8
Esprit	--	--	22583	37.2	22583	30.6
Formula	--	--	14519	22.0	14519	19.7
Trans Am	--	--	10255	10.4	10255	13.9
Total	7603	10.3	66126	89.7	73729	100.0

DRIVETRAIN DATA

Standard base model:	D
Cylinder Configuration:	Inline
Number of Cylinders:	6
Cylinder Bore (in):	3.875
Cylinder Stroke (in):	3.53
Displacement (cu in):	249.8
Carburetion:	1 1-bbl
Carburetor Make:	Rochester
Carburetor Model:	MV
Compression Ratio:	8.25
Brake Horsepower (net):	100
RPM @ Maximum Hp:	3600
Torque, ft-lb (net):	175
RPM @ Maximum Torque:	1800

Esprit standard:	M	Option base:	M
Cylinder Configuration:	V	Standard formula:	M
Number of Cylinders:	8	Cylinder Configuration:	V
Cylinder Bore (in):	3.875	Number of Cylinders:	8
Cylinder Stroke (in):	3.75	Cylinder Bore (in):	3.875
Displacement (cu in):	353.8	Cylinder Stroke (in):	3.75
Carburetion:	1 2-bbl	Displacement (cu in):	353.8
Carburetor Make:	Rochester	Carburetion:	1 2-bbl
Carburetor Model:	2GV	Carburetor Make:	Rochester
Compression Ratio:	7.6	Carburetor Model:	2GV
Brake Horsepower (net):	155	Compression Ratio:	7.6
(170 in Formula 350)		Brake Horsepower (net):	170
RPM @ Maximum Hp:	3600	RPM @ Maximum Hp:	3600
(3600 in Formula 350)		(3600 in Formula 350)	
Torque, ft-lb (net):	275	Torque, ft-lb (net):	275
(290 in Formula 350)		(290 in Formula 350)	
RPM @ Maximum Torque: 2400		RPM @ Maximum Torque: 2400	

Esprit option:	R	Option Formula:	R
Cylinder Configuration:	V	Cylinder Configuration:	V
Number of Cylinders:	8	Number of Cylinders:	8
Cylinder Bore (in):	4.12	Cylinder Bore (in):	4.12
Cylinder Stroke (in):	3.75	Cylinder Stroke (in):	3.75
Displacement (cu in):	400.0	Displacement (cu in):	400.0
Carburetion:	1 2-bbl	Carburetion:	1 2-bbl
Carburetor Make:	Rochester	Carburetor Make:	Rochester
Carburetor Model:	2GV	Carburetor Model:	2GV
Compression Ratio:	8.0	Compression Ratio:	8.0
Brake Horsepower (net): (190 in Formula 400)	175	Brake Horsepower (net): (190 in Formula 400)	190
RPM @ Maximum Hp: (4000 in Formula 400)	3600	RPM @ Maximum Hp: (4000 in Formula 400)	3600
Torque, ft-lb (net): (330 in Formula 400)	315	Torque, ft-lb (net): (330 in Formula 400)	315
RPM @ Maximum Torque: (4000 in Formula 400)	2000	RPM @ Maximum Torque: (4000 in Formula 400)	2000

Option Formula & Standard Trans Am:	S	Option Formula & Trans Am	W
Cylinder Configuration:	V	Cylinder Configuration:	V
Number of Cylinders:	8	Number of Cylinders:	8
Cylinder Bore (in):	4.12	Cylinder Bore (in):	4.151
Cylinder Stroke (in):	3.75	Cylinder Stroke (in):	4.206
Displacement (cu in):	400.0	Displacement (cu in):	455.4
Carburetion:	1 4-bbl	Carburetion:	1 4-bbl
Carburetor Make:	Rochester	Carburetor Make:	Rochester
Carburetor Model:	4MV	Carburetor Model:	4MV
Compression Ratio:	8.0	Compression Ratio:	8.0
Brake Horsepower (net):	225	Brake Horsepower (net):	250
RPM @ Maximum Hp:	4000	RPM @ Maximum Hp:	4000
Torque, ft-lb (net):	330	Torque, ft-lb (net):	380
RPM @ Maximum Torque:	2800	RPM @ Maximum Torque:	2800

Trans Am option:	X	Option Formula:	X
Cylinder Configuration:	V	Cylinder Configuration:	V
Number of Cylinders:	8	Number of Cylinders:	8
Cylinder Bore (in):	4.151	Cylinder Bore (in):	4.151
Cylinder Stroke (in):	4.206	Cylinder Stroke (in):	4.206
Displacement (cu in):	455.4	Displacement (cu in):	455.4
Carburetion:	1 4-bbl	Carburetion:	1 4-bbl
Carburetor Make:	Rochester	Carburetor Make:	Rochester
Carburetor Model:	4MV	Carburetor Model:	4MV
Compression Ratio:	8.4	Compression Ratio:	8.4
Brake Horsepower (net):	290	Brake Horsepower (net):	290
RPM @ Maximum Hp:	4000	RPM @ Maximum Hp:	4000
Torque, ft-lb (net):	395	Torque, ft-lb (net):	395
RPM @ Maximum Torque:	3200	RPM @ Maximum Torque:	3200

TRANSMISSIONS

Engine Hp:	100	155	175	225	250	290
Standard:	3-spdM	3-spdM	3-spdM	4-speed	4-spdM	4-spdM
Optional:	4-spdM	4-spdM	4-spdM	3-spdA	3-spdA	3-spdA
	3-spdA	3-spdA	3-spdA			

Transmission Ratios

	3-spdM			4-spdM			3-spdA	
first:	2.85	2.54*	2.54	2.52#	2.20+		2.52	2.48#
second:	1.68	1.50*	1.80	1.88#	1.64+		1.52	1.48#
third:	1.00	1.00*	1.44	1.46#	1.28+		1.00	1.00#
fourth:	--	--	1.00	1.00#	1.00+		--	--
reverse:	2.95	2.63*	2.54	2.59#	2.27+		1.92	2.08

* 350 cid; # 400/455 cid; + 455 cid

Rear Axle Ratios
standard all models: 3.08
4-spd TA standard: 3.42

EXTERIOR DATA

Overall Length (in):	196.0
Overall Width (in):	73.4
Overall Height (in):	50.4
Wheelbase (in):	108.0

Shipping Weight (lb):

base	Esprit	Formula	Trans Am
3283	3540	3548	3655

EXTERIOR FINISHES

Color	Code	Color	Code
Starlight Black	A	Cameo White	C
Porcelain Blue	D	Admiralty Blue	E
Regatta Blue	F	Carmel Beige	G
Denver Gold	H	Limefire Green	J
Gulfmist Aqua	K	Lakemist Green	L
Fernmist Green	M	Pinemist Green	N
Buccaneer Red	R	Honduras Maroon	S
Sunstorm Yellow	T	Shadowmist Brown	U
Ascot Silver	V	Fire Coral Bronze	W
Colonial Gold	Y	Crestwood Brown	Z

UPHOLSTERY

Material	Color	Code	Recommended Exterior Colors
Morrokide	White	721	C,E,F,G,H,J,K,M,N,R,S,T,V,W,Y,Z
	Saddle	731	C,G,H,J,S,T,V,W,Z
	Black	761	C,E,F,G,H,J,K,M,N,R,S,T,V,W,Y,Z
	Blue	811*	C,E,F
	Red	901*	C,E,R,V
	White	921*	C,E,F,G,H,J,K,M,N,R,S,T,V,W,Y,Z
	Saddle	931*	C,G,H,J,S,T,V,W,Z
	Green	941*	C,J,M,N
	Black	961*	C,E,F,G,H,J,K,M,N,R,S,T,V,W,Y,Z

Cloth/Morrokide Saddle   831* C,G,H,J,S,T,V,W,Z
                 Black   461* C,D,E,F,H,J,K,L,M,R,S,T,U,V,Y,Z
                 Burgundy 471* C,E,S
                 Beige   551* C,E,H,J,K,L,M,R,S,T,U,V,Y,Z

Mixed Color Interiors

Seat Color	Code	Interior Color
White	331	Black (761)
Red	338	Black (761)
Blue	335	White (721)
Green	336	White (721)
Red	338	White (721)
Red	331*	Blue (811)
White	331*	Red (901)
White	331*	Green (941)
White	331*	Black (961)
Black	332*	Red (901)
Red	333*	Black (961)

Appointment Color#

Blue	335*	White (921)
Green	336*	White (921)
Red	338*	White (921)
Red	338*	Black (861)
Red	338*	Black (961)

#Carpeting, instrument panel, steering column, package shelf
*Custom interiors extra cost on Formula and Trans Am

PRICE DATA

base	Esprit	Formula	Formula 400	Trans Am	Trans Am Standard 455
3175	3527	3614	3721	4401	4923

CURRENT VALUE (approximate)

Model Condition	Best	Very Good	Good	Fair	Poor
base	2700	1890	1350	810	405
Esprit	2900	2030	1450	870	435
Formula	7500	5250	3750	2250	1125
Trans Am	9300	6510	4650	2790	1395

POPULAR FACTORY OPTIONS

Item	Code	Price (nearest $)	
Air-conditioning	582	412	
Clock, Electric	711	15	
Console	431	58	
Console, rear	424	26	
Differential, Safe-T-Track	371	45	
Engine, 400	L78	97	(std on TA)
Engine, 455	L75	154	(57 on TA)
Engine, SD 455	LS2	675	(578 on TA)
Glass, Tinted	571	38	
Glass, Tinted, windshield only	572	31	
Hood Decal	512	55	(TA only)
Hood, Ram Air	514	56	(Formula 400 or 455 only)
Instruments, Rally & Clock	712	46	
Instruments, Rally, Clock & Tach	714	92	
Mirrors 2, left remote control	434	26	
Power Brakes, Disc	502	49	
Power Door Locks	554	46	
Power Windows	551	78	(req.console)
Radio, Pushbutton	411	65	
Radio, AM/FM	413	135	
Radio, AM/FM Stereo	415	233	

Rear Speaker	421	18	
Rear Window Defogger	594	33	
Rear Window Defroster	592	64	
Seat Belts, custom front & rear	691	15	
Spare Tire, Space-Saver	684	15	
Steering Wheel, Formula	464	56	
Steering Wheel, tilt	504	46	
Tape, 8-track	422	130	
Transmission, 4-speed M	M20	206	
Transmission, 3-speed A	M38	211	
Wheels Discs, custom finned	472	50	(24, Esprit)
Wheel Discs, deluxe	476	26	
Wheel Discs, Honeycomb	478	123	(97, Esprit)
Wheels, Rally II	474	87	(61, Esprit)

PERFORMANCE DATA

Source:	MOTOR TREND	WORLD CAR	AUTO GUIDE 74
Engine Hp:	175	250	290
Transmission:	3-spdA	3-spdA	3-spdA
Rear Axle Ratio:	3.08	3.08	3.08
0 to 60 Time (sec):	10.35	nr	6.4
1/4 Mile Time (sec):	17.052	nr	14.3
1/4 Mile Speed (mph):	82.11	nr	101
Maximum Speed (mph):	nr	130	127
60 to 0 Braking Distance (ft):	139.6	nr	nr
MPG (city):	nr	nr	nr
MPG (highway):	nr	nr	nr
MPG (combined):	nr	10.7	8.3

nr = not reported
*from 70 mph

1975

Physical Features

Revisions to the grillework differentiated the 1975 Firebird from its predecessor. Thin horizontal bars were used and the parking lights were placed in the outer ends of the grilles. The same engines were offered, but the larger V-8s were not available in as many versions. The 400 cid motor was rated at 185 hp and the 455 was reduced to 200 hp. There were no options available with either engine. For the first time, the 6-cylinder motor was available in the Esprit.

Observations

While industry sales of North American cars fell nearly 8%, Firebird ignored that trend and sold 18% more cars than the year before. Firebird's share of Pontiac's total sales climbed to 16% despite the introduction of the economical Astre to meet the demands of the market when fuel supplies were limited and rising sharply in cost. Evidently, the Firebird was catching the attention of a segment of the public that was not reacting to the energy crisis. Leading Firebird's popularity was the Trans Am. Its 1975 total was more than the number of base models built for 1974. Production of the Trans Am jumped over 2.5 times its record total of the year before. It climbed so fast that, by the end of the 1975 model year, 55% of all Trans Ams ever built were 1975 models.

Firebird

VIN NUMBERS

Vehicle Identification Number: 2( )87( )( )5( )100001 and up
Explanation:
First symbol: GM division: Pontiac = 2
Second symbol: Series number:
base Firebird = S
    Esprit = T
    Formula = U
    Trans Am = V
Third & fourth symbols: Body code: coupe = 87
Fifth symbol: Letter indicating engine:
    D = 105 hp
    M = 155 hp
    R = 175 hp
    S = 185 hp
    Y = 260 hp
Sixth symbol: Last digit of model year
Seventh symbol: Letter indicating assembly plant
Eighth to thirteenth symbols:
    Sequential production number starting with 100001

PRODUCTION TOTALS

Model	Total	%	Transmission Installations		
base	26372	35.8	3-spdM	2347	2.8
Esprit	22583	30.6	4-spdM	10775	12.8
Formula	14519	19.7	3-spdA	70941	84.4
Trans Am	10255	13.9			
Total	73729	100.0			

	Units	%
6 cyl	8314	9.9
V-8	75749	90.1

Trans Am Engine/Transmission Installations

Engine	4-spdM	%	3-spdA	%
400 cid	6140	22.5	20277	74.3
455 cid	–	–	857	3.1

DRIVETRAIN DATA

Standard base model:	D		Standard Esprit:	D
Cylinder Configuration:	Inline		Cylinder Configuration:	Inline
Number of Cylinders:	6		Number of Cylinders:	6
Cylinder Bore (in):	3.875		Cylinder Bore (in):	3.875
Cylinder Stroke (in):	3.53		Cylinder Stroke (in):	3.53
Displacement (cu in):	249.8		Displacement (cu in):	249.8
Carburetion:	1 1-bbl		Carburetion:	1 1-bbl
Carburetor Make:	Rochester		Carburetor Make:	Rochester
Carburetor Model:	1MY		Carburetor Model:	1MY
Compression Ratio:	8.25		Compression Ratio:	8.25
Brake Horsepower (net):	105		Brake Horsepower (net):	105
RPM @ Maximum Hp:	3800		RPM @ Maximum Hp:	3800
Torque, ft-lb (net):	185		Torque, ft-lb (net):	185
RPM @ Maximum Torque:	1200		RPM @ Maximum Torque:	1200

Esprit standard:	M		Firebird base:	M
Cylinder Configuration:	V		Cylinder Configuration:	V
Number of Cylinders:	8		Number of Cylinders:	8
Cylinder Bore (in):	3.875		Cylinder Bore (in):	3.875
Cylinder Stroke (in):	3.75		Cylinder Stroke (in):	3.75
Displacement (cu in):	353.8		Displacement (cu in):	353.8
Carburetion:	1 2-bbl		Carburetion:	1 2-bbl
Carburetor Make:	Rochester		Carburetor Make:	Rochester
Carburetor Model:			Carburetor Model:	
Compression Ratio:	7.6		Compression Ratio:	7.6
Brake Horsepower (net):	155		Brake Horsepower (net):	155
RPM @ Maximum Hp:	4000		RPM @ Maximum Hp:	4000
Torque, ft-lb (net):	280		Torque, ft-lb (net):	280
RPM @ Maximum Torque:	2000		RPM @ Maximum Torque:	2000

Formula standard:	E	Firebird & Esprit option:	E
Cylinder Configuration:	V	Cylinder Configuration:	V
Number of Cylinders:	8	Number of Cylinders:	8
Cylinder Bore (in):	3.875	Cylinder Bore (in):	3.875
Cylinder Stroke (in):	3.75	Cylinder Stroke (in):	3.75
Displacement (cu in):	353.4	Displacement (cu in):	353.4
Carburetion:	1 4-bbl	Carburetion:	1 4-bbl
Carburetor Make:	Rochester	Carburetor Make:	Rochester
Carburetor Model:	M4MC	Carburetor Model:	M4MC
Compression Ratio:	7.6	Compression Ratio:	7.6
Brake Horsepower (net):	175	Brake Horsepower (net):	175
RPM @ Maximum Hp:	4000	RPM @ Maximum Hp:	4000
Torque, ft-lb (net):	280	Torque, ft-lb (net):	280
RPM @ Maximum Torque:	2000	RPM @ Maximum Torque:	2000

Trans Am standard:	S	Option Formula:	S
Cylinder Configuration:	V	Cylinder Configuration:	V
Number of Cylinders:	8	Number of Cylinders:	8
Cylinder Bore (in):	4.12	Cylinder Bore (in):	4.12
Cylinder Stroke (in):	3.75	Cylinder Stroke (in):	3.75
Displacement (cu in):	400.0	Displacement (cu in):	400.0
Carburetion:	1 4-bbl	Carburetion:	1 4-bbl
Carburetor Make:	Rochester	Carburetor Make:	Rochester
Carburetor Model:	M4MC	Carburetor Model:	M4MC
Compression Ratio:	7.6	Compression Ratio:	7.6
Brake Horsepower (net):	185	Brake Horsepower (net):	185
RPM @ Maximum Hp:	3600	RPM @ Maximum Hp:	3600
Torque, ft-lb (net):	310	Torque, ft-lb (net):	310
RPM @ Maximum Torque:	1600	RPM @ Maximum Torque:	1600

Trans Am option:	Y
Cylinder Configuration:	V
Number of Cylinders:	8
Cylinder Bore (in):	4.151
Cylinder Stroke (in):	4.206
Displacement (cu in):	455.4
Carburetion:	1 4-bbl
Carburetor Make:	Rochester
Carburetor Model:	M4MCA
Compression Ratio:	7.6
Brake Horsepower (net):	200
RPM @ Maximum Hp:	3500
Torque, ft-lb (net):	330
RPM @ Maximum Torque:	2000

TRANSMISSIONS

Engine Hp:	105	155	175	185	200
Standard:	3-spdM	4-spdM	4-spdM	4-spdM	4-spdM
Optional:	3-spdA	3-spdA	3-spdA	3-spdA	3-spdA

Transmission Ratios

	3-spdM	4-spdM*	4-spdM#	3-spdA
first:	2.85	2.54	2.43	2.52
second:	1.68	1.80	1.61	1.52
third:	1.00	1.46	1.23	1.00
fourth:	--	1.00	1.00	--
reverse:	2.95	2.59	2.35	1.92

*with 350 cid; # with 400 & 455 cid

Rear Axle Ratios

	base	Esprit	Formula	Trans Am
std:	2.73	2.73	3.08*	3.08

*2.56 in California

EXTERIOR DATA

Overall Length (in):   196.0
Overall Width (in):   73.0
Overall Height (in):   49.1
Wheelbase (in):   108.1
Shipping Weight (lb):

base	Esprit	Formula	Trans Am
3386	3655	3631	3716

EXTERIOR FINISHES

Color	Code	Color	Code
Cameo White	C	Arctic Blue	D
Stellar Blue	E	Bimini Blue	F
Carmel Beige	G	Sandstone	H
Ginger Brown	J	Lakemist Green	L
Alpine Green	M	Honduras Maroon	P
Buccaneer Red	R	Sunstorm Yellow	T
Sterling Silver	V	Graystone	W
Copper Mist	Y	Persimmon	Z

UPHOLSTERY

Material	Color	Code	Recommended Exterior Colors
Morrokide	Black	19V1	C,D,E,F,G,H,J,L,M,P,R,T,V,W,Y,Z
	White	11V1	C,D,E,F,G,H,J,L,M,P,R,T,V,W,Y,Z
	Saddle	63V1	C,G,H,J,L,M,T,W,Y,Z
	Black	19W1*	C,D,E,F,G,H,J,L,M,P,R,T,V,W,Y,Z
	White	11W1*	C,D,E,F,G,H,J,L,M,P,R,T,V,W,Y,Z
	Saddle	63W1*	C,G,H,J,L,M,T,W,Y,Z
	Blue	26W1*	C,D,E,F,V
	Burgundy	73W1*	C,P,V,W

Mixed Interiors Seat Color	Code	Interior Color	Recommended Exterior Color
White	91V1	Black/White	C,D,E,F,G,H,J,L,M,P,R,T, V,W,Y,Z
White	96V1	Saddle/White	C,G,H,J,L,M,T,W,V,Z
White	92W1*	Blue/White	C,D,E,F,V
White	91W1*	Black/White	C,D,E,F,G,H,J,L,M,P,R,T, V,W,Y,Z
White	97W1*	Burgundy/White	C,P,V,W
White	96W1*	Saddle/White	C,G,H,J,L,M,T,W,Y,Z

Appt.Color#	Code	Recommended Exterior Color
White/Blue	11V1/346	C,D,E,F,V
White/Burgundy	11V1/347	C,P,V,W
Black/Burgundy	19V1/347	C,P,V,W
White/Saddle	11V1/343	C,G,H,J,L,M,T,W,Y,Z
White/Burgundy	11W1/347*	C,P,V,W
White/Blue	11W1/346*	C,D,E,F,V
White/Saddle	11W1/343*	C,G,H,J,L,M,T,W,Y,Z
Burgundy/Black	73W1/349*	C,P,V,W
Black/Burgundy	19W1/347*	C,P,V,W

#Carpeting, instrument panel, steering column, package shelf
*Custom interiors, extra cost on Formula and Trans Am

PRICE DATA

base	Esprit	Formula	Formula 400	Trans Am
3713	3958	4349	4684	4740

CURRENT VALUE (approximate)

Model Condition	Best	Very Good	Good	Fair	Poor
base	2400	1680	1200	720	360
Esprit	2600	1820	1300	780	390
Formula	3900	2730	1950	1170	585
Trans Am	8200	5740	4100	2460	1230

POPULAR FACTORY OPTIONS

Item	Code	Price (nearest $)	
Air-conditioning	582	435	
Clock, Electric	711	16	
Console	431	68	
Console, rear	424	41	
Differential, Safe-T-Track	581	49	
Glass, Tinted	571	43	
Hood Decal	512	55	(TA only)
Instruments, Rally & Clock	712	50	
Instruments, Rally, Clock & Tach	714	99	
Mirrors 2, left remote control	422	27	(base only)
Power Brakes, Disc	502	55	
Power Door Locks	554	56	
Power Windows	551	91	(req.console)
Radio, Pushbutton	401	69	
Radio, AM/FM	403	135	
Radio, AM/FM Stereo	405	233	
Rear Speaker	412	130	
Rear Window Defogger	594	41	
Rear Window Defroster	592	70	
Seat Belts, custom front & rear	441	19	
Steering Wheel, Custom	461	16	(base only)
Steering Wheel, Formula	464	57	(41 Esprit & Formula)
Steering Wheel, tilt	504	49	
Tape, 8-track	412	130	(req.console)
Transmission, 4-speed M	M20	219	(base & Esprit)
Transmission, 3-speed A	M38	237	(base & Esprit)
Vinyl Roof	PVT	99	
Wheels Discs, deluxe	476	30	
Wheel Discs, custom finned	472	54	(24, Esprit)
Wheel Discs, Honeycomb	478	127	(77, Esprit)
Wheels, Rally II	474	91	(61, Esprit)

PERFORMANCE DATA

Source:	WORLD CAR	MOTOR TREND	CAR & DRIVER
Engine Hp:	175	185	200
Transmission:	3-spdA	3-spdA	4-spdM
Rear Axle Ratio:	3.08	3.08	3.23
0 to 60 Time (sec):	nr	9.8	7.8
1/4 Mile Time (sec):	nr	16.75	16.1
1/4 Mile Speed (mph):	nr	84.98	88.8
Maximum Speed (mph):	118	nr	118
70 to 0 Braking Distance (ft):	nr	nr	191
MPG (city):	nr	nr	12.0
MPG (highway):	nr	nr	12.5
MPG (combined):	12.1	16.59	nr

nr = not reported
*from 70 mph

Physical Features

Deeply set honeycomb mesh was the new grille identification for 1976. That and the return of the parking lights to
below the bumper were the main external changes. An optional appearance package for the Formula included a wide
decal for the sills and bottom edge of the fenders. In large
letters, the word "Formula" identified the model. Even
though the convertible had long ago disappeared, a new
approach to open-air touring came in the form of a T-Top,
removable roof panels over the front seat. This was only
available on the Trans Am and was part of the Limited
Edition option offered to celebrate Pontiac's 50th anniver-
sary. The Limited Edition models were black with gold trim
and gold honeycomb wheels. Engines were little changed.

Observations

Firebird was on a tremendous roll. There seemed to be no
end to demand for these great cars. Sales climbed another
28%. The Firebird portion of total Pontiac sales dropped to
14% due to increased popularity of the other Pontiac lines.
Firebird's popularity was led again by its best performing
and highest priced model, the Trans Am. Incidentally, prices
were rising rather fast, but there seemed to be little evidence
of consumer resistance. To meet its demand, Trans Am production was increased over 70% to more than 46,700. That
meant there were more 1976 Trans Ams built than 1973
Firebirds of all models.

Firebird Formula

VIN NUMBERS

Vehicle Identification Number: 2( )87( )( )6( )100001 and up
Explanation:
First symbol: GM division: Pontiac = 2
Second symbol: Series number:
base Firebird = S
   Esprit = T
   Formula = U
   Trans Am = V
Third & fourth symbols: Body code: coupe = 87
Fifth symbol: Letter indicating engine:
   D = 110 hp
   M = 160 hp
   J = 165 hp
   Z = 185 hp
   W = 200 hp
Sixth symbol: Last digit of model year
Seventh symbol: Letter indicating assembly plant
Eighth to thirteenth symbols:
   Sequential production number starting with 100001

PRODUCTION TOTALS

Model	Total	%
base	21209	19.1
Esprit	22252	20.1
Formula	20613	18.6
Trans Am	46701	42.2
Total	110775	100.0

	Units	%
6 cyl	9405	8.5
V-8	101370	91.5

Transmission Installations

3-spdM	2456	2.2
4-spdM	15952	14.4
3-spdA	92367	83.4

Limited Edition Trans Am

Engine	T-Top	%	Non-T-Top	%
400 cid	533	20.6	319	12.3
455 cid	110	4.2	1628	62.9
Total	643	24.8	1947	75.2

Trans Am Engine/Transmission Installations

Engine	4-spdM	%	3-spdA	%
400 cid	5424	11.6	33752	72.3
455 cid	7528	16.1	–	16.1

Limited Edition Trans Am

Engine	T-Top	%	Non-T-Top	%
400 cid	533	20.6	319	12.3
455 cid	110	4.2	1628	62.9
Total	643	24.8	1947	75.2

DRIVETRAIN DATA

Standard base model:	D		Standard Esprit:	D
Cylinder Configuration:	Inline		Cylinder Configuration:	Inline
Number of Cylinders:	6		Number of Cylinders:	6
Cylinder Bore (in):	3.875		Cylinder Bore (in):	3.875
Cylinder Stroke (in):	3.53		Cylinder Stroke (in):	3.53
Displacement (cu in):	249.8		Displacement (cu in):	249.8
Carburetion:	1 1-bbl		Carburetion:	1 1-bbl
Carburetor Make:	Rochester		Carburetor Make:	Rochester
Carburetor Model:	1MV		Carburetor Model:	1MV
Compression Ratio:	8.25		Compression Ratio:	8.25
Brake Horsepower (net):	110		Brake Horsepower (net):	110
RPM @ Maximum Hp:	3800		RPM @ Maximum Hp:	3800
Torque, ft-lb (net):	185		Torque, ft-lb (net):	185
RPM @ Maximum Torque:	1200		RPM @ Maximum Torque:	1200
Option Firebird base:	M		Esprit standard Formula:	M
Cylinder Configuration:	V		Cylinder Configuration:	V
Number of Cylinders:	8		Number of Cylinders:	8
Cylinder Bore (in):	3.875		Cylinder Bore (in):	3.875
Cylinder Stroke (in):	3.75		Cylinder Stroke (in):	3.75
Displacement (cu in):	353.8		Displacement (cu in):	353.8
Carburetion:	1 2-bbl		Carburetion:	1 2-bbl
Carburetor Make:	Rochester		Carburetor Make:	Rochester

Carburetor Model:		Carburetor Model:	
Compression Ratio:	7.6	Compression Ratio:	7.6
Brake Horsepower (net):	160	Brake Horsepower (net):	160
RPM @ Maximum Hp:	4000	RPM @ Maximum Hp:	4000
Torque, ft-lb (net):	280	Torque, ft-lb (net):	280
RPM @ Maximum Torque:	2000	RPM @ Maximum Torque:	2000

Formula standard:	E	Option base Esprit &	
Cylinder Configuration:	V	Formula*	E
Number of Cylinders:	8	Cylinder Configuration:	V
Cylinder Bore (in):	3.875	Number of Cylinders:	8
Cylinder Stroke (in):	3.75	Cylinder Bore (in):	3.875
Displacement (cu in):	353.4	Cylinder Stroke (in):	3.75
Carburetion:	1 4-bbl	Displacement (cu in):	353.4
Carburetor Make:	Rochester	Carburetion:	1 4-bbl
Carburetor Model:	M4MC	Carburetor Make:	Rochester
Compression Ratio:	7.6	Carburetor Model:	M4MC
Brake Horsepower (net):	165	Compression Ratio:	7.6
RPM @ Maximum Hp:	4000	Brake Horsepower (net):	165
Torque, ft-lb (net):	280	RPM @ Maximum Hp:	4000
RPM @ Maximum Torque:	2000	Torque, ft-lb (net):	280
		RPM @ Maximum Torque:	2000

*California only with automatic transmission

Standard Trans Am:	S	Option Esprit:	S
Cylinder Configuration:	V	Cylinder Configuration:	V
Number of Cylinders:	8	Number of Cylinders:	8
Cylinder Bore (in):	4.12	Cylinder Bore (in):	4.12
Cylinder Stroke (in):	3.75	Cylinder Stroke (in):	3.75
Displacement (cu in):	400.0	Displacement (cu in):	400.0
Carburetion:	1 4-bbl	Carburetion:	1 4-bbl
Carburetor Make:	Rochester	Carburetor Make:	Rochester
Carburetor Model:	M4MC	Carburetor Model:	M4MC
Compression Ratio:	7.6	Compression Ratio:	7.6
Brake Horsepower (net):	185	Brake Horsepower (net):	185
RPM @ Maximum Hp:	3600	RPM @ Maximum Hp:	3600
Torque, ft-lb (net):	310	Torque, ft-lb (net):	310
RPM @ Maximum Torque:	1600	RPM @ Maximum Torque:	1600

Trans Am option:	W
Cylinder Configuration:	V
Number of Cylinders:	8
Cylinder Bore (in):	4.151
Cylinder Stroke (in):	4.206
Displacement (cu in):	455.4
Carburetion:	1 4-bbl
Carburetor Make:	Rochester
Carburetor Model:	M4MC
Compression Ratio:	7.6
Brake Horsepower (net):	200
RPM @ Maximum Hp:	3500
Torque, ft-lb (net):	330
RPM @ Maximum Torque:	2000

TRANSMISSIONS

Engine Hp:	110	160	165	185	200
Standard:	3-spdM	3-spdA	3-spdA	4-spdM	4-spdM
Optional:	3-spdA			3-spdA	3-spdA

Transmission Ratios

	3-spdM	4-spdM	4-spdM*	3-spdA
first:	2.85	2.43	2.20	2.52
second:	1.68	1.61	1.64	1.52
third:	1.00	1.23	1.28	1.00
fourth:	--	1.00	1.00	–
reverse:	2.95	2.35	2.27	1.92

*Optional on Trans Am in addition to other 4-spdM

Rear Axle Ratios

	base	Esprit	Formula	Trans Am
std:	3.08	3.08	2.56	3.08
opt:	–	–	–	3.23

EXTERIOR DATA

Overall Length (in):   196.8
Overall Width (in):   73.0
Overall Height (in):   49.1
Wheelbase (in):   108.1
Shipping Weight (lb):

base	Esprit	Formula	Trans Am
3383	3431	3625	3640

EXTERIOR FINISHES

Color	Code	Color	Code
Cameo White*	C	Sterling Silver*	V
Starlight Black*	A	Athena Blue	D
Polaris Blue	E	Firethorn Red*	R
Cordova Maroon	P	Metalime Green	B
Alpine Green	M	Baravian Cream	G
Goldenrod Yellow*	T	Buckskin Tan	H
Durango Bronze	Y	Carousel Red*	N

*available on Trans Am

UPHOLSTERY

Material	Color	Code	Recommended Exterior Color
Morrokide	Black	19M1	any color
	White	11M1	any color
	Buckskin	64M1	A,C,G,H,M,N,P,R,T,Y
	Firethorn	71N1	A,C,P,R,V
	Blue	26N1	A,C,D,E

Mixed Interiors Seat Color	Code	Interior Color	Recommended Exterior Color
White	91N1	Firethorn/White	A,C,P,R,V
White	92N1	Blue/White	A,C,D,E
White	97N1	Black/White	A,B,C,D,E,G,H,M,N,P,R,T,V,Y

Appt.Color#	Code	Recommended Exterior Color
White/Blue	11M1/341	A,C,D,E
White/Firethorn	11M1/343	A,C,P,R,V
White/Lime	11M1/344	A,B,C
White/Blue	11N1/341*	A,C,D,E
White/Firethorn	11N1/343*	A,C,P,R,V
White/Lime	11N1/344*	A,B,C

*Custom interiors, extra cost on Formula and Trans Am
#Carpeting, instrument panel, steering column, package shelf

PRICE DATA

base	Esprit	Formula	Formula 400	Trans Am
3906	4162	4566	4684	4987

CURRENT VALUE (approximate)

Model Condition	Best	Very Good	Good	Fair	Poor
base	2400	1680	1200	720	360
Esprit	2600	1820	1300	780	390
Formula	3600	2520	1800	1080	540
Trans Am	7400	5180	3700	2220	1110

POPULAR FACTORY OPTIONS

Item	Code	Price (nearest dollar)	
Air-conditioning	492	452	
Clock, Electric	474	18	
Console	581	71	
Console, rear	572	43	
Differential, Safe-T-Track	391	51	
Glass, Tinted	442	46	
Hood Decal	564	58	(TA only)
Instruments, Rally & Clock	502	54	
Instruments, Rally, Clock & Tach	504	106	

Mirrors 2, left remote control	642	29	
Power Brakes, Disc	452	58	
Power Door Locks	434	62	
Power Windows	431	99	
Radio, Pushbutton	411	92	
Radio, AM/FM	413	153	
Radio, AM/FM Stereo	415	233	
Rear Speaker	421	20	
Rear Window Defogger	462	48	
Rear Window Defroster	461	77	
Seat Belts, custom front & rear	524	20	
Steering Wheel, Custom	541	17	
Steering Wheel, tilt	444	43	(60, base)
Transmission, 4-speed M	M21	242	
Transmission, 3-speed A	M38	262	
Wheels Discs, deluxe	556	32	
Wheel Discs, Honeycomb	558	135	(103, Esprit)
Wheels, Rally II	559	113	(81, Esprit)

PERFORMANCE DATA

Source:	WORLD CAR	WORLD CAR	CAR & DRIVER
Engine Hp:	165	185	200
Transmission:	3-spdA	4-spdM	4-spdM
Rear Axle Ratio:	2.41	3.08	3.23
0 to 60 Time (sec):	nr	nr	7.0
1/4 Mile Time (sec):	nr	nr	15.6
1/4 Mile Speed (mph):	nr	nr	90.3
Maximum Speed (mph):	112	118	117.6
70 to 0 Braking Distance (ft):	nr	nr	175
MPG (city):	nr	nr	12.0
MPG (highway):	nr	nr	13.0
MPG (combined):	18	16.8	nr

nr = not reported

Firebird Formula

Physical Features

There was a substantial change made to the front end
design of the 1977 Firebird. The very slanted front had
the appearance of the hood coming down to a point at the
bumper. Actually, the grille shape was similar to the top half
of the 1959 Pontiac grille. Dual rectangular headlights were
situated in the outer ends of the grille. The same models were
offered as well as the Special Edition option on the Trans
Am. There were several major engine changes. The Chevrolet six was discarded in favor of Buick's V-6 which developed about the same power. This was standard in the base
and Esprit models. A new Pontiac engine with a 301 cid
displacement became the standard engine for the Formula
Firebird. The 350 V-8 continued as an Esprit and Formula
option but not in California. For that state, a different 350
from Chevrolet was installed with similar power ratings. For
the Trans Am, the 400 V-8 remained as standard power.
There was no 455 engine any more, so a more powerful version of the 400, called the 400 T/A, was offered. Neither of
these engines were sold in California. Trans Am buyers there
were given an Oldsmobile engine with a 403 displacement
which was rated about the same as the standard Pontiac 400.
That 403 was teamed with a 3-speed automatic transmission
with no other choice.

Observations

Firebird popularity raged unabated. Registrations during
calendar 1977 climbed over 35% to capture 17% of all Pontiac sales. Production had to keep pace of course, and the
Trans Am was the undisputed Firebird favorite. More 1977
Trans Ams were built than base and Esprit models combined
and their production totals were the highest thus far despite
substantial price increases.

VIN NUMBERS

Vehicle Identification Number: 2( )87( )( )7( )100001 and up
Explanation:
First symbol: GM division: Pontiac = 2
Second symbol: Series number:
base Firebird = S
    Esprit = T
    Formula = U
    Trans Am = W
Third & fourth symbols: Body code: coupe = 87
Fifth symbol: Letter indicating engine:
    C = 105 hp
    Y = 135 hp
    L = 170 hp
    R = 170 hp (California)
    Z = 180 hp
    F = 200 hp
    K = 185 hp (California)
Sixth symbol: Last digit of model year
Seventh symbol: Letter indicating assembly plant
Eighth to thirteenth symbols:
    Sequential production number starting with 100001

PRODUCTION TOTALS

Model	Total	%
base	30642	19.7
Esprit	34548	22.2
Formula	21801	14.0
Trans Am	68745	44.1
Total	155736	100.0

	Units	%
6 cyl	15080	9.7
V-8	140656	90.3

Transmission Installations

3-spdM	953	0.6
4-spdM	14015	9.0
3-spdA	140768	90.4

Trans Am Engine/Transmission Installations

Engine	4-spdM	%	3-spdA	%
180 hp	–	–	36092	52.5
200 hp	11402	16.6	14775	21.5
185 hp	–	–	6476	9.4

Special Edition Engine/Transmission with T-Top

180 hp	–	–	6030	38.7
200 hp	2699	17.3	3760	24.2
185 hp	–	–	1217	7.8

Without T-Top

180 hp	–	–	748	4.8
200 hp	384	2.5	549	3.5
185 hp	–	–	180	1.2

DRIVETRAIN DATA

Standard base model:	LD7
Cylinder Configuration:	V
Number of Cylinders:	6
Cylinder Bore (in):	3.8
Cylinder Stroke (in):	3.4
Displacement (cu in):	231.4
Carburetion:	1 2-bbl
Carburetor Make:	Rochester
Carburetor Model:	2GC
Compression Ratio:	8.0
Brake Horsepower (net):	105
RPM @ Maximum Hp:	3200
Torque, ft-lb (net):	185
RPM @ Maximum Torque:	2000

Standard Firebird base & Esprit	LD7
Cylinder Configuration:	V
Number of Cylinders:	6
Cylinder Bore (in):	3.8
Cylinder Stroke (in):	3.4
Displacement (cu in):	231.4
Carburetion:	1 2-bbl
Carburetor Make:	Rochester
Carburetor Model:	2GC
Compression Ratio:	8.0
Brake Horsepower (net):	105
RPM @ Maximum Hp:	3200
Torque, ft-lb (net):	185
RPM @ Maximum Torque:	2000

Formula standard:	L27
Cylinder Configuration:	V
Number of Cylinders:	8
Cylinder Bore (in):	4.0
Cylinder Stroke (in):	3.0
Displacement (cu in):	301.6
Carburetion:	1 2-bbl
Carburetor Make:	Rochester
Carburetor Model:	M2MC200
Compression Ratio:	8.2
Brake Horsepower (net):	135
RPM @ Maximum Hp:	4000
Torque, ft-lb (net):	245
RPM @ Maximum Torque:	2000

Option base & Esprit standard Formula	L27
Cylinder Configuration:	V
Number of Cylinders:	8
Cylinder Bore (in):	4.0
Cylinder Stroke (in):	3.0
Displacement (cu in):	301.6
Carburetion:	1 2-bbl
Carburetor Make:	Rochester
Carburetor Model:	M2MC200
Compression Ratio:	8.2
Brake Horsepower (net):	135
RPM @ Maximum Hp:	4000
Torque, ft-lb (net):	245
RPM @ Maximum Torque:	2000

Formula option*:	L76
Cylinder Configuration:	V
Number of Cylinders:	8
Cylinder Bore (in):	4.0
Cylinder Stroke (in):	3.48
Displacement (cu in):	349.8
Carburetion:	1 4-bbl
Carburetor Make:	Rochester
Carburetor Model:	M4MC
Compression Ratio:	8.5
Brake Horsepower (net):	170
RPM @ Maximum Hp:	3800
Torque, ft-lb (net):	270
RPM @ Maximum Torque:	2400

*Option all series except Trans Am

California*:   L34
Cylinder Configuration: V
Number of Cylinders: 8
Cylinder Bore (in):   4.057
Cylinder Stroke (in):   3.385
Displacement (cu in):   350.1
Carburetion: 1 4-bbl
Carburetor Make: Rochester
Carburetor Model: M4MC
Compression Ratio: 7.9
Brake Horsepower (net):   170
RPM @ Maximum Hp: 3800
Torque, ft-lb (net):   275
RPM @ Maximum Torque: 2000

*California option all series except Trans Am

Trans Am standard:	L78	Option Formula:	L78
Cylinder Configuration:	V	Cylinder Configuration:	V
Number of Cylinders:	8	Number of Cylinders:	8
Cylinder Bore (in):	4.12	Cylinder Bore (in):	4.12
Cylinder Stroke (in):	3.75	Cylinder Stroke (in):	3.75
Displacement (cu in):	400.0	Displacement (cu in):	400.0
Carburetion:	1 4-bbl	Carburetion:	1 4-bbl
Carburetor Make:	Rochester	Carburetor Make:	Rochester
Carburetor Model:	M4MC	Carburetor Model:	M4MC
Compression Ratio:	7.6	Compression Ratio:	7.6
Brake Horsepower (net):	180	Brake Horsepower (net):	180
RPM @ Maximum Hp:	3600	RPM @ Maximum Hp:	3600
Torque, ft-lb (net):	325	Torque, ft-lb (net):	325
RPM @ Maximum Torque:	1600	RPM @ Maximum Torque:	1600

Trans Am option:	W72
Cylinder Configuration:	V
Number of Cylinders:	8
Cylinder Bore (in):	4.12
Cylinder Stroke (in):	3.75
Displacement (cu in):	400.0
Carburetion:	1 4-bbl
Carburetor Make:	Rochester
Carburetor Model:	M4MC
Compression Ratio:	8.0
Brake Horsepower (net):	200
RPM @ Maximum Hp:	3600
Torque, ft-lb (net):	325
RPM @ Maximum Torque:	2400

Option Formula & Trans Am:	W72
Cylinder Configuration:	V
Number of Cylinders:	8
Cylinder Bore (in):	4.12
Cylinder Stroke (in):	3.75
Displacement (cu in):	400.0
Carburetion:	1 4-bbl
Carburetor Make:	Rochester
Carburetor Model:	M4MC
Compression Ratio:	8.0
Brake Horsepower (net):	200
RPM @ Maximum Hp:	3600
Torque, ft-lb (net):	325
RPM @ Maximum Torque:	2400

California Trans Am:	?
Cylinder Configuration:	V
Number of Cylinders:	8
Cylinder Bore (in):	4.351
Cylinder Stroke (in):	3.385
Displacement (cu in):	402.6
Carburetion:	1 4-bbl
Carburetor Make:	Rochester
Carburetor Model:	M4MC
Compression Ratio:	8.0
Brake Horsepower (net):	185
RPM @ Maximum Hp:	3600
Torque, ft-lb (net):	320
RPM @ Maximum Torque:	2200

Standard Trans Am option Formula*	?
Cylinder Configuration:	V
Number of Cylinders:	8
Cylinder Bore (in):	4.351
Cylinder Stroke (in):	3.385
Displacement (cu in):	402.6
Carburetion:	1 4-bbl
Carburetor Make:	Rochester
Carburetor Model:	M4MC
Compression Ratio:	8.0
Brake Horsepower (net):	185
RPM @ Maximum Hp:	3600
Torque, ft-lb (net):	320
RPM @ Maximum Torque:	2200

*In California only

TRANSMISSIONS

Engine Hp:	105	135	170	180	200/185
Standard:	3-spdM	4-spdM	3-spdA	4-spdM	4-spdM*
Optional:	4-spdM	3-spdA		3-spdA	3-spdA
	3-spdA				

*Not available with 185 hp

Transmission Ratios

	3-spdM	4-spdM*	4-spdM#	3-spdA
first:	3.11	2.85	2.43	2.52
second:	1.84	2.02	1.75	1.52
third:	1.00	1.35	1.47	1.00
fourth:	--	1.00	1.00	–
reverse:	3.22	2.85	2.35	1.92

*With 301 cid
#With 400 cid

Rear Axle Ratios

	std.Fed.	std.Cal.
Base, Esprit	3.08	3.23
Formula	2.41	2.41
Trans Am	2.41	2.41

EXTERIOR DATA

Overall Length (in): 196.8
Overall Width (in): 73.0
Overall Height (in): 49.1
Wheelbase (in): 108.1
Shipping Weight (lb):

base	Esprit	Formula	Trans Am
3264	3312	3411	3526

EXTERIOR FINISHES

Color	Code	Color	Code
Cameo White*	11	Sterling Silver*	13
Starlight Black*	19	Lombard Blue**	21
Glacier Blue	22	Nautilus Blue	29
Firethorn Red	36	Aquamarine	38
Bahia Green	44	Goldenrod Yellow*	51
Gold Metallic	55	Bright Blue	58
Mojave Tan	61	Buckskin Metallic	63
Brentwood Brown*	75	Buccaneer Red*	75
Manderin Orange	78		

*Available on Trans Am

**Available on Skybird standard

UPHOLSTERY

Material	Color	Code	Recommended Exterior Colors
Vinyl	White	11R1	any color
	Black	19R1	any color
	Buckskin	64R1	11,19,44,51,61,63,69,78
	Firethorn	71R1	11,13,19,36
	White	11N1*	any color
	Black	19N1*	any color
	Blue	24N1*	11,19,22,29
	Buckskin	64N1*	11,19,44,51,61,63,69,78
	Firethorn	71N1*	11,13,19,36
Cloth	Black	19B1*	any color
	Blue	24B1*	11,19,22,29
	Firethorn	71B1*	11,13,19,36

Mixed Interiors Seat Color	Code	Interior Color	Recommended Exterior Color
White	97R1	Firethorn/White	11,13,19,36
White	92N1*	Blue/White	11,19,22,29
White	97N1*	Firethorn/White	11,13,19,36

Appt.Color#	Code	Recommended Exterior Color
White/Blue	11R1/26X	11,19,22,29
White/Turquoise	11R1/34X	11,19,38
White/Saddle	11R1/64X	11,19,44,51,61,63,69,78
White/Firethorn	11R1/71X	11,13,19,36
White/Blue	11N1/26X*	11,19,22,29
White/Turquoise	11N1/34X*	11,19.38
White/Saddle	11N1/64X*	11,19,22,29
White/Firethorn	11N1/71X*	11,13,19,36

*Custom interiors, extra cost on Formula and Trans Am
#Carpeting, instrument panel, steering column, package shelf

PRICE DATA

base	Esprit	Formula	Trans Am
4270	4551	4977	5456

CURRENT VALUE (approximate)

Model Condition	Best	Very Good	Good	Fair	Poor
base	2400	1680	1200	720	360
Esprit	2600	1820	1300	780	390
Formula	3300	2310	1650	990	495
Trans Am	6500	4550	3250	1950	975

POPULAR FACTORY OPTIONS

Item	Code	Price (nearest $)
Air-conditioning	C60	478
Clock, Electric	U35	21
Console	D55	75
Console, rear	D58	46
Deck Lid Release, remote control	A90	18
Differential, Safe-T-Track	G80	54

Engine, 400 cid	L78	155	
Engine, 403 cid	L80	155	
Formula Appearance Package	W50	127	
Glass, Tinted	A01	50	
Handling Package, Rally RTS	QCY	115	
Hood Decal	WW7	62	
Instruments, Rally & Clock	W63	60	
Instruments, Rally, Clock & Tach	WW8	116	
Mirrors 2, left remote control	D35	31	
Power Brakes, Disc	JL2	61	
Power Door Locks	AU3	68	
Power Windows	A31	108	
Radio, Pushbutton	U63	79	
Radio, AM/FM	U69	137	
Radio, AM/FM Stereo	U58	233	
Rear Air Spoiler	D80	51	
Rear Speaker	U80	23	
Rear Window Defroster	C49	82	
Seat Belts, custom front & rear	AK1	21	
Skybird Appearance Package	W60	385	
Special Edition Trans Am w/hatch roof	Y82	1143	(w/out, 556)
Steering Wheel, Formula	NK3	61	
Steering Wheel, tilt	N33	57	
Steering Wheel, Luxury	N30	18	
Tape, 8-track	U57	134	
Transmission, 4-speed M	M20	257	
Transmission, 3-speed A	M40	282	
Wheels Discs, deluxe	P01	34	
Wheel Discs, wire	N95	134	(100, Esprit)
Wheel Discs, cast aluminum	YJ8	227	(193, Esprit)
Wheels, Rally II	N98	106	(72, Esprit)

PERFORMANCE DATA

Source:	WORLD CAR	WORLD CAR	ROAD TEST
Engine Hp:	170	180	200
Transmission:	3-spdA	3-spdA	4-spdM
Rear Axle Ratio:	2.41	3.23	3.23
0 to 60 Time (sec):	nr	nr	8.7
1/4 Mile Time (sec):	nr	nr	16.9
1/4 Mile Speed (mph):	nr	nr	83.2
Maximum Speed (mph):	109	115	115
60 to 0 Braking Distance (ft):	nr	nr	nr
MPG (city):	nr	nr	nr
MPG (highway):	nr	nr	nr
MPG (combined):	18	17	16

nr = not reported
*from 70 mph

Trans Am

Physical Features

Very little change for the 1978 Firebirds was visible from the exterior. The same models continued and the Special Edition Trans Am was repeated with gold replacing black as the color in midyear. Both had a T-roof. An option for the Esprit with a special finish was the Redbird which was replaced in midyear by the Bluebird. Changes made under the hood included the replacement of the Pontiac 301 V-8 by a 305 Chevrolet V-8. Horsepower was increased except in the California version. While the Oldsmobile 403 V-8 remained virtually unchanged, there was a Chevrolet 350 of slightly less power installed for Californians. The big engines remained the same as before, except that the optional 400 cid V-8 got 10% more horsepower.

Observations

Firebird continued its sales spectacular, chalking up a 30% increase in registrations. Production increased, but only by 20%. The Trans Am continued its climb in popularity. Practically half the 1978 Firebird model run was made up of the much-desired Trans Am. Two production milestones were passed during the year. Shortly before 1978 production ended, the 1,000,000th Firebird was built. About the same time, the 250,000th Trans Am came off the assembly line. Those two facts combined indicate the great favor the Trans Am had earned.

VIN NUMBERS

Vehicle Identification Number: 2( )87( )( )8( )100001 and up
Explanation:
First symbol: GM division: Pontiac = 2
Second symbol: Series number:
  base Firebird = S
  Esprit = T
  Formula = U
  Trans Am = W
Third & fourth symbols: Body code: coupe = 87
Fifth symbol: Engine code:
  A = 105 hp
  U = 145/135 hp
  L = 170 hp
  R = 160 hp (for California)
  Z = 180/220 hp
  K = 185 hp (for California)
Sixth symbol: Last digit of model year
Seventh symbol: Letter indicating assembly plant
Eighth to thirteenth symbols:
  Sequential production number starting with 100001

PRODUCTION TOTALS

Model	Units	%
base	32672	17.4
Esprit	36926	19.7
Formula	24346	13.0
Trans Am	93341	49.8
Total	187285	100.0*

*May not total 100 due to rounding

Engine Installations

6 cyl	13595	7.3
V-8	173690	92.7

Transmission Installations

3-spdM	1622	0.9
4-spdM	18021	9.6
3-spdA	167642	89.5

Trans Am Engine/Transmission Installations

Engine	4-spdM	%	3-spdA	%	Total	%
180 hp	8553	9.2	66092	71.2	75031	80.4
200 hp	4112	4.4	4139	4.4	8251	8.8
185 hp	–	–	10059	10.8	10059	10.8

Special Edition (black) Engine/Transmission Installations

180/200 hp	509	4.1	2924	23.8
185 hp	–	–	210	1.7
Special Edition (gold)				
180/200 hp	1267	10.3	6519	53.0
185 hp	–	–	880	7.1

DRIVETRAIN DATA

base model, standard:	LD5	Standard Firebird base	
Cylinder Configuration:	V	& Esprit:	LD5
Number of Cylinders:	6	Cylinder Configuration:	V
Cylinder Bore (in):	3.8	Number of Cylinders:	6
Cylinder Stroke (in):	3.4	Cylinder Bore (in):	3.8
Displacement (cu in):	231.4	Cylinder Stroke (in):	3.4
Carburetion:	1 2-bbl	Displacement (cu in):	231.4
Carburetor Make:	Rochester	Carburetion:	1 2-bbl
Carburetor Model:	2GE	Carburetor Make:	Rochester
Compression Ratio:	8.0	Carburetor Model:	2GE
Brake Horsepower (net):	105	Compression Ratio:	8.0
RPM @ Maximum Hp:	3200	Brake Horsepower (net):	105
Torque, ft-lb (net):	185	RPM @ Maximum Hp:	3200
RPM @ Maximum Torque:	2000	Torque, ft-lb (net):	185
		RPM @ Maximum Torque:	2000

Formula standard:	LG3	Option base & Esprit:	LG3
Cylinder Configuration:	V	Cylinder Configuration:	V
Number of Cylinders:	8	Number of Cylinders:	8
Cylinder Bore (in):	3.74	Cylinder Bore (in):	3.74
Cylinder Stroke (in):	3.48	Cylinder Stroke (in):	3.48
Displacement (cu in):	305.8	Displacement (cu in):	305.8
Carburetion:	1 2-bb	Carburetion:	1 2-bbl 1
Carburetor Make:	Rochester	Carburetor Make:	Rochester
Carburetor Model:	2GC	Carburetor Model:	2GC
Compression ratio:	8.4	Compression ratio:	8.4
Brake Horsepower (net):	145	Brake Horsepower (net):	145
(135 with A/T)		(135 with A/T)	
RPM @ Maximum Hp:	3800	RPM @ Maximum Hp:	3800
Torque, ft-lb (net):	245	Torque, ft-lb (net):	245
(240 with A/T)		(240 with A/T)	
RPM @ Maximum Torque:	2400	RPM @ Maximum Torque:	2400

Formula option*:	LM1
Cylinder Configuration:	V
Number of Cylinders:	8
Cylinder Bore (in):	4.0
Cylinder Stroke (in):	3.48
Displacement (cu in):	349.8
Carburetion:	1 4-bbl
Carburetor Make:	Rochester
Carburetor Model:	M4MC
Compression Ratio:	8.5
Brake Horsepower (net):	170
RPM @ Maximum Hp:	3800
Torque, ft-lb (net):	270
RPM @ Maximum Torque:	2400

*Option all series except Trans Am

Trans Am standard:	L78
Cylinder Configuration:	V
Number of Cylinders:	8
Cylinder Bore (in):	4.12
Cylinder Stroke (in):	3.75
Displacement (cu in):	400.0
Carburetion:	1 4-bbl
Carburetor Make:	Rochester
Carburetor Model:	M4MC
Compression Ratio:	7.7
Brake Horsepower (net):	180
RPM @ Maximum Hp:	3600
Torque, ft-lb (net):	325
RPM @ Maximum Torque:	1600

Option Formula:	L78
Cylinder Configuration:	V
Number of Cylinders:	8
Cylinder Bore (in):	4.12
Cylinder Stroke (in):	3.75
Displacement (cu in):	400.0
Carburetion:	1 4-bbl
Carburetor Make:	Rochester
Carburetor Model:	M4MC
Compression Ratio:	7.7
Brake Horsepower (net):	180
RPM @ Maximum Hp:	3600
Torque, ft-lb (net):	325
RPM @ Maximum Torque:	1600

Trans Am option:	W72	Option Formula &	
Cylinder Configuration:	V	Trans Am:	W72
Number of Cylinders:	8	Cylinder Configuration:	V
Cylinder Bore (in):	4.12	Number of Cylinders:	8
Cylinder Stroke (in):	3.75	Cylinder Bore (in):	4.12
Displacement (cu in):	400.0	Cylinder Stroke (in):	3.75
Carburetion:	1 4-bbl	Displacement (cu in):	400.0
Carburetor Make:	Rochester	Carburetion:	1 4-bbl
Carburetor Model:	M4MC	Carburetor Make:	Rochester
Compression Ratio:	8.1	Carburetor Model:	M4MC
Brake Horsepower (net):	220	Compression Ratio:	8.1
RPM @ Maximum Hp:	4000	Brake Horsepower (net):	220
Torque, ft-lb (net):	320	RPM @ Maximum Hp:	4000
RPM @ Maximum Torque:	2800	Torque, ft-lb (net):	320
		RPM @ Maximum Torque:	2800

Trans Am (California):	L80	Option Formula & Trans Am*	
Cylinder Configuration:	V	standard Trans Am**:	L80
Number of Cylinders:	8	Cylinder Configuration:	V
Cylinder Bore (in):	4.351	Number of Cylinders:	8
Cylinder Stroke (in):	3.385	Cylinder Bore (in):	4.351
Displacement (cu in):	402.6	Cylinder Stroke (in):	3.385
Carburetion:	1 4-bbl	Displacement (cu in):	402.6
Carburetor Make:	Rochester	Carburetion:	1 4-bbl
Carburetor Model:	M4MC	Carburetor Make:	Rochester
Compression Ratio:	7.9	Carburetor Model:	M4MC
Brake Horsepower (net):	185	Compression Ratio:	7.9
RPM @ Maximum Hp:	3600	Brake Horsepower (net):	185
Torque, ft-lb (net):	320	RPM @ Maximum Hp:	3600
RPM @ Maximum Torque:	2000	Torque, ft-lb (net):	320
		RPM @ Maximum Torque:	2000

*High altitude & California
**California

TRANSMISSIONS

Engine Hp:	105	145/135	170/160	180	220	185
Standard:	3-spdM	3-spdM*	3-spdA	3-spdA	3-spdA	3-spdA
Optional:	3-spdA	3-spdA	4-spdM	4-spdM	4-spdM	

Transmission Ratios

	3-spdM	4-spdM*	4-spdM#	3-spdA
first:	3.11	2.85	2.43	2.52
second:	1.84	2.02	1.61	1.52
third:	1.00	1.35	1.23	1.00
fourth:	--	1.00	1.00	--
reverse:	3.22	2.85	2.35	1.92

* with 305/350 cid
# with 400 cid

Rear Axle Ratios

Engine Hp:	105	145	170	180	220	170*	185*
Standard:	2.56	2.29	2.41	2.41	3.23	2.41	2.41
Optional:	2.73	2.41	2.73	2.56	3.42	2.73	2.56
	2.93	2.56	3.08	3.08			2.73
	3.08	2.73		3.23			3.08
	3.23	3.08					

*California

EXTERIOR DATA

Overall Length (in):	196.8
Overall Width (in):	73.4
Overall Height (in):	49.3
Wheelbase (in):	108.1

Shipping Weight (lb):

base	Esprit	Formula	Trans Am
3254	3285	3452	3511

EXTERIOR FINISHES

Color	Code	Color	Code
Cameo White	11	Platinum	15
Starlight Black	19	Glacier Blue*	22
Martinique Blue	24	Lombard Blue**	30
Solar Gold#	50	Berkshire Green	48
Laredo Brown*	63	Sundance Yellow	51
Chesterfield Brown	69	Ember Mist*	67
Carmine*	77	Mayan Red	75
		Roman Red***	72

*Not available on Trans Am; **Skybird only; #Trans Am only
***Red Bird only

UPHOLSTERY

Material	Color	Code	Recommended Exterior Colors
Vinyl	Oyster	12R1	any color
	Black	19R1	any color
	Camel Tan	62R1	11,19,50,51,63,69,77
	Carmine	74R1	11,15,19,77
	Oyster	12N1*	any color
	Black	19N1*	any color
	Blue	24N1*	11,15,22,24
	Camel Tan	62N1*	11,19,50,51,63,69,77
	Firethorn	74N1*	11,15,19,77
Cloth	Black	19B1*	any color
	Blue	24B1*	11,15,22,24
	Camel Tan	62B1*	11,19,50,51,63,69,77
	Carmine	74B1*	11,15,19,77

Mixed Color Interiors			Recommended
Appt. Color#	Code	Code	Exterior Color
Oyster/Gray	12R1/16X	12N1/16X*	any color
Oyster/Black	12R1/19X	12N1/19X*	any color
Oyster/Blue	12R1/24X	12N1/24X*	11,15,22,24
Oyster/Camel Tan	12R1/61X	12N1/62X*	11,50,63,69

*Custom interiors, extra cost on Formula and Trans Am
#Carpeting, instrument panel, steering column, package shelf

PRICE DATA

base	Esprit	Formula	Trans Am
4593	4897	5533	5889

CURRENT VALUE (approximate)

Model Condition	Best	Very Good	Good	Fair	Poor
base	2500	1750	1250	750	375
Esprit	2700	1890	1350	810	405
Formula	3000	2100	1500	900	450
Trans Am	5500	3850	2750	1650	825

POPULAR FACTORY OPTIONS

Item	Code	Price (nearest $)
Air-conditioning	C60	508
Canopy Top	CB7	111
Clock, Electric	U35	22
Console	D55	80
Deck Lid Release, remote control	A90	21
Differential, Safe-T-Track	G80	60
Engine, 400 cid	W72	280
Engine, 403 cid	L80	205
Formula Appearance Package	W50	137
Glass, Tinted	A01	56
Hatch Roof, removable glass panels	CC1	625
Hood Decal	WW7	66
Instruments, Rally & Clock	W63	63
Instruments, Rally, Clock & Tach	WW8	123
Mirrors, 2, left remote control	D35	34
Power Brakes, Disc	JL2	69
Power Door Locks	AU3	80
Power Windows	A31	124
Radio, pushbutton	U63	83
Radio, AM/FM	U69	154
Radio, AM/FM Stereo	U58	236

Radio, AM/FM Stereo & Cassette	UN3	351	
Radio, AM/FM Stereo & 8-track	UM2	341	
Rear Deck Spoiler	D80	55	
Rear Speaker	U80	24	
Rear Window Defroster	C49	92	
Red Bird Appearance Package	W68	430	
Seat Belts, custom front & rear	AK1	21	
Skybird Appearance Package	W60	461	
Special Edition Trans Am Appearance Package	Y82	1259	
Steering Wheel, Formula	NK3	65	
Steering Wheel, Luxury	N30	19	
Steering Wheel, tilt	N33	69	
Trans Am Special Performance Package	WS6	324	
Transmission, 3-speed A	MX1	307	
Transmission, 4-speed M	MM4	125	
Wheel Discs, Deluxe	P01	38	
Wheel Discs, wire	N95	146	(108, Esprit)
Wheels, cast aluminum	YJ8	290	(252, Esprit)
Wheels, Rally II	N98	117	(79, Esprit)
Windshield Wipers, pulse	CD4	32	

PERFORMANCE DATA

Source:	WORLD CAR	WORLD CAR	WORLD CAR
Engine Hp:	170	220	185
Transmission:	4-spdM	4-spdM	3-spdA
Rear Axle Ratio:	3.08	3.42	2.56
0 to 60 Time (sec):	nr	nr	nr
1/4 Mile Time (sec):	nr	nr	nr
1/4 Mile Speed (mph):	nr	nr	nr
Maximum Speed (mph):	103	118	112
60 to 0 Braking Distance (ft):	nr	nr	nr
MPG (city):	nr	nr	nr
MPG (highway):	nr	nr	nr
MPG (combined):	nr	nr	nr

nr = not reported